Sefer A Journey into Holiness

Stories of Tzaddikim

Written by
Reb Moshe Steinerman

Edited by Elise Teitelbaum

A Journey into Holiness

ilovetorah Jewish Outreach Network

ilovetorah Jewish Publishing
First Published 2018
ISBN: 978-1-947706-05-7

Editors: Elise Teitelbaum & Rochel Steinerman

Artwork by Boris Shapiro

ABOUT THE AUTHOR

Rabbi Moshe Steinerman grew up as a religious Jew on the hillsides of Maryland. During his teenage years, Reb Moshe developed his talent for photography, while connecting to nature and speaking to *Hashem*. He later found his path through *Breslev chassidus*, while maintaining closeness to the *litvish* style of learning. He studied in the Baltimore yeshiva, *Ner Yisrael*, then married, and moved to Lakewood, New Jersey. After settling down, he began to write his first book, Kavanos Halev, with the blessing of Rav Malkiel Kotler *Shlita, Rosh Yeshiva* of *Beis Medresh Gevoha*.

After establishing one of the first Jewish outreach websites, ilovetorah.com in 1996, Reb Moshe's teachings became popular amongst the full spectrum of Jews, from the unaffiliated to ultra-Orthodox. His teachings, including hundreds of stories of tzaddikim, gained popularity due to the ideal of drawing Jews together. Reb Moshe made *aliyah* to Tzfat, Israel in 2003. Since then he has helped to bring back thousands of English-speaking Jews to their Jewish roots, through his hundreds of online Jewish videos and audio shiurim. His learning experience includes the completion of both Talmud Bavli and Yerushalmi as well as other important works.

In 2012, Reb Moshe, with his wife and children, moved to Jerusalem. Some of his other books are Kavanos Halev, Tikkun Shechinah, Tovim Meoros (Glimpse of Light), Chassidus, Kabbalah & Meditation, Yom Leyom (Day by Day), Prayers of the Heart, Pesukei Torah (Passages of Torah), and The True Intentions of the Baal Shem Tov. Thousands have read the advice contained in these books, with life-changing results.

---

*In Memory of my father, Shlomo
Zavel Ben Yaakov ZT"L, My father-in-law
Menachem Ben Reuven ZT"L
And all the great souls of our
people*

I grew up in a house filled with the Torah learning of my father, who studied most of the day. Although there were no Jews in this remote part of Maryland, my father was a man of chesed to all people and was known for his brilliance in Torah scholarship.

I want to say a special thank you to the Nikolsberg Rebbe and the Biala Rebbe for their encouragement and blessings. Most of all, I offer thanks to my wife, Rochel, for her faithful support.

---

*Dedicated to my wife Rochel
and to my children Shlomo
Nachman, Yaakov Yosef, Gedalya Aharon
Tzvi, Esther Rivka, Yeshiya Michel, Dovid
Shmuel, Eliyahu Yisrael
may it bring forth the light of your
neshamos.*

Dear Reader,

Ilovetorah Jewish Outreach is an online, non-profit organization, where books and *Torah* classes are available at low cost. Therefore, we appreciate your donation to help Rabbi Moshe Steinerman, and ilovetorah.com, in order to help them continue their work on behalf of the Jewish people. We also ask that you pass on these books to others once you are finished with them.

Thank you,
Reb Moshe Steinerman
www.ilovetorah.com
www.ilovetorah.com/donations

RABBINIC APPROVALS / HASKAMAHS

בס״ד

RABBI DOVID B. KAPLAN
RABBI OF WEST NEW YORK
5308 PALISADE AVENUE • WEST NEW YORK, NJ 07093
201-867-6859 • WESTNEWYORKSHUL@GMAIL.COM

דוד ברוך הלוי קאפלאן
רב ואב״ד דק״ק
וועסט ניו יארק

י' שבט ה'תשע"ז / February 6, 2017

Dear Friends,

Shalom and Blessings!

For approximately twenty years I have followed the works of Rabbi Moshe Steinerman, Shlit"a, a pioneer in the use of social media to encourage people and bring them closer to G-d.

Over the years Rabbi Steinerman has produced, and made public at no charge, hundreds of videos sharing his Torah wisdom, his holy stories, and his touching songs. Rabbi Steinerman has written a number of books, all promoting true Jewish Torah spirituality. Rabbi Steinerman's works have touched many thousands of Jews, and even spirituality-seeking non-Jews, from all walks of life and at all points of the globe.

Rabbi Steinerman is a tomim (pure-hearted one) in the most flattering sense of the word.

I give my full approbation and recommendation to all of Rabbi Steinerman's works.

I wish Rabbi Steinerman much success in all his endeavors.

May G-d bless Rabbi Moshe Steinerman, his wife, Rebbetzin Rochel Steinerman, and their beautiful children; and may G-d grant them health, success, and nachas!

With blessings,

Rabbi Dovid B. Kaplan

7

Rabbi M. Lebovits

Grand Rabbi of
Nikolsburg

53 Decatur Avenue
Spring Valley, N.Y. 10977

יוסף יחיאל מיכל
לעבאוויטש
ניקלשבורג

מאנסי - ספרינג וואלי, נ.י.

בעזהשי"ת

בשורותי אלו באתי להעיד על מעשה אומן, מופלא מופלג בהפלגת חכמים ונבונים,
ירא וחרד לדבר ה', ומשתוקק לקרב לבות ישראל לאביהם שבשמים,
ה"ה הרב **משה שטיינערמאן** שליט"א בעיה"ק צפת תובב"א

שעלה בידו להעלות על הספר נפלאים שאסף מספרים הקדושים, בענין אהבה
אחוה שלום וריעות, לראות מעלות חברינו ולא חסרונם, יעי"ז להיות נמנעים מדברי
ריבות ומחלוקת, ולתקן עון שנאת חנם אשר בשביל זה נחרב בית מקדישינו
ותפארתינו, וכמשאחז"ל (ירושי' ויקרא רבה פ' כ') על ויחן שם ישראל. שניתנה תורה באופן
שחנו שם כאיש אחד בלב אחד.

וניכר בספר כי עמל ויגע הרבה להוציא מתחת ידי דבר נאה ומתוקן, ע"כ אף ידי תבון
עמו להוציא לאור עולם. ויהי רצון שחפץ ה' בידו יצליח, ויברך ה' חילו ופועל ידי
תרצה, שיברך על המוגמר להגדיל תורה ולהאדירה ולהפיצן בקרב ישראל, עד ביאת
גוא"צ בב"א

א"ד הכותב לכבוד התורה ומרביציה,
י"ט חשון תשפ"ו

Approval of the Biala Rebbe of New York / Betar / Miami

הובא לפני גליונות בעניני קירוב רחוקים לקרב אחינו בני ישראל אל
אביהם שבשמים, כידוע מהבעש"ט זיע"א שאמר "אימתי קאתי מר
לכשיפוצו מעינותיך חוצה" ואפריון נמטי"ה להאי גברא יקירא מיקירי
צפת עיה"ק תובב"א כמע"כ מוהר"ר משה שטיינרמן שליט"א אשר כבר
עוסק רבות בשנים לקרב רחוקים לתורה וליהדות, וכעת מוציא לאור
ספר בשם "דרך לקדושה" וראיתי דברים נחמדים מאוד וניכר מתוך
הדברים שהרב בעל המחבר - אהבת השי"ת ואהבת התורה וישראל
בלבבו, ובטחוני כי הספר יביא תועלת גדולה לכל עם ישראל.

ויה"ר שיזכה לבוא לגומרה ברוב פאר והדר ונזכה לגאולתן של ישראל
בב"א.

בכבוד רב:
אהרן שלמה חיים אליעזר
בלאאו"ר הללה"ה אב'שא

Rabbi Abraham Y. S. Friedman
161 Maple Avenue #C Spring Valley NY 10977
Tel: 845-425-5043 Fax: 845-425-8045

אברהם יחזקאל שרגא פרידמאן
רב דביהמ"ד אמרי"י שפ"ר קאסאדא
וראש כולל יצרי"

בעזהשי"ת

ישפות השם החיים והשלו', לכבוד ידידי מאז ומקדם מיקירי קרתא
דירושלים יראה שלם, זוכה ומזכה אחרים, להיות דבוק באלקינו, ה"ה
הר"ר משה שטיינרמאן שליט"א.

שמחתי מאוד לשמוע ממך, מאתר רחוק וקירוב הלבבות, בעסק
תורתך הקדושה ועבודתך בלי לאות, וכה יעזור ה' להלאה ביתר שאת
ויתר עז, והנה שלחת את הספר שלקטת בעניני דביקות בה', לקרב
לבבות בני ישראל לאבינו שבשמים בשפת אנגלית, אבל דא עקא
השפת לא ידענו, ע"כ לא זכיתי לקרותו, ע"כ א"א לי ליתן הסכמה פרטי
על ספרך, ובכלל קיבלתי על עצמי שלא ליתן הסכמות, ובפרט כשאין
לי פנאי לקרות הספר מתחלתו עד סופו, אבל בכלליות זכרתי לך חסד
נעוריך, היאך הי' המתיקות שלך בעבדות השם פה בעירינו, ובנועם
המדות, והזקה על חבר שאינו מוציא מתחת ידו דבר שאינו מתוקן,
ובפרט שכל מגמתך להרבות כבוד שמים, שבוודאי סייעתא דשמיא
ילוך כל ימיך לראות רב נחת מיוצ"ח ומפרי ידיך, שתתקבל הספר
בסבר פנים יפות אצל אחינו בני ישראל שמדברים בשפת האנגלית
שיתקרבו לאבינו שבשמים ולהדבק בו באמת כאות נפשך, ולהרבות
פעלים לתורה ועבודה וקדושה בדביקות עם מדות טובות, בנייחותא
נייחא בעליונים ונייחא בתחתונים עד ביאת גואל צדק בב"א.

כ"ד ידידך השמח בהצלחתך ובעבודתך

אברהם יחזקאל שרגא פרידמאן

אבד"ק קאסאדא

Table of Contents

Introduction

Some say that taking time out to read stories of *tzaddikim* could be construed as a waste of one's time. Time in which could otherwise be used for *Torah* study. However, that isn't the case, as stories of our sages have the ability to awaken our souls in unexpected ways.

The Rambam says that speaking highly of the great qualities of *tzaddikim* is highly beneficial, as it encourages one to follow their ways. Rabbeinu Yonah writes that praising *tzaddikim* is tantamount to praising *Hashem* and doing so brings out the good within the speaker. (פיהמ"ש אבות א,טז, שערי תשובה שער ג)

The Ba'al HaTanya explained that *sippurei tzaddikim* are an important supplement to learning *Torah* because they lead to *yiras Shamayim*. Hearing or reading inspiring stories encourages a person to upgrade his *Torah* learning, his *yiras Shamayim*, and lead him to serve *Hashem lishmah*, for His sake alone.

We heard from the Ba'al Shem Tov, "When one recounts the praises of the *tzaddikim*, it was as if he engages in the mysteries of the *Ma'aseh Merkavah*." (Shiv'chei Ba'al Shem Tov *158*)

He also said that every day a person should tell one of his friends a story about the deeds of a *tzaddik*. Therefore, I hope through this holy book of stories, you can daily find something inspiring to help you and a friend through their day.

The Power of Stories

Some hope

In the *beis medrash* of R' Chaim of Sanz, it was the custom to learn *Torah* late into the night. In fact, it was something that the *rebbe* expected of his closest students since there is no time more conducive for productive *Torah* learning than the night.

One late night, after many hours of uninterrupted study, the students felt weary. They commenced to *schmooze* amongst themselves. When *Torah* scholars start *schmoozing* they don't talk about just any subject! What do they talk about? Stories of the *tzaddikim*, the righteous and holy *rebbes* who founded and fostered the *chassidic* movement.

As they were talking, suddenly R' Chaim walked into the study hall. Immediately he perceived that the students had already left off studying. "And what is this *schmoozing* about," he challenged them. Embarrassed as they were, they had no alternative but to "confess." The eldest of the group found the courage to stammer, "We..we..we..were tr...tr..trading stories of *tza..tza..addikim*."

"Is that so?" demurred the *rebbe*.

"Then I also have a story to share."

"There once was, maybe there still is, a huge bird who lived on a desert isle and his name is the Fah. The Fah was stricken with painful and unseemly sores all over his legs. At times, he would look at his legs and sink into utter desperation because of the terrible sores, and he would contemplate hurling himself into the sea. Finally, he decides to take off into flight, and prepare himself for his final moments, before hurtling into the depths. As his last minute of life approaches, he suddenly catches a glimpse of his outstretched wings, skillfully maneuvering the air currents, their multicolored feathers glistening and glimmering in the sunlight. He feels unexpectedly revived, his desire for life surges through him, and the Fah changes course, now soaring higher and higher into the skies with a new enthusiasm and joy.

"So, it is with us," R' Chaim said. "When we glance at ourselves and our deeds we can easily come to despair. How small and insignificant we are! How much potential have we wasted. How many precious hours and minutes have we let slip through our fingers with nothing accomplished. But, when we tell stories of our *tzadikkim*, and reflect on their lives and deeds, we become refreshed. We remember just what a Jew can become. We once again have hope!"

Not Just After Shabbos

The Maharash of Lubavitch once said, "People say that relating a story of the Ba'al Shem Tov on *motzei Shabbos* is a segula for *parnasah*. The truth is that it does not necessarily have to be about the Ba'al Shem Tov, it can be about any *tzaddik*. Secondly, it is not only applicable on *motzei Shabbos*, but also at any, and all times. Lastly, the segula is not only for *parnasah* – but for all good things as well."

Stories as a Segula

Before the Ba'al HaTanya relayed *divrei Torah* from the Ba'al Shem Tov, he would remark, "The words of *Torah* from 'the *zeide*' (as he called the Ba'al Shem Tov) are a *segulah* to increase one's understanding, and in achieving true *yiras Shamayim*. Relating stories of 'the *zeide*' are a *segulah* for long life and abundant *parnasah*." When the daughter of the Tzemach Tzedek once fell ill with high fever, he recommended that someone read her stories of the Ba'al Shem Tov, for "they are a superb *segulah* to heal fever."

A Story First

The prominent *chassid* and *gaon* Reb Aizik, Rov of Homel, was sent by his *rebbe,* the Tzemach Tzedek, to Ruzhin in order to attend to a public matter. Reb Aizik used the opportunity to observe the ways of the Ruzhiner *chassidim* and of their saintly *rebbe*, Reb Yisroel. He observed that two *chassidim* came to Ruzhin to receive the *rebbe's haskamah* for *seforim* they had written. One book was filled with *chiddushei Torah,* and the other recounted *sippurim* of *tzaddikim* and *chassidim* of note. The *rebbe* requested that part of each *sefer* be read out loud. After sitting in *d'veikus* for a while, he suddenly praised the telling of *sippurei tzaddikim,* a pursuit in this world that arouses echoes in the *heichalos* of *tzaddikim* in *Olam Habah*. Then, the *rebbe* presented a *pilpul* on some of the *chiddushei Torah* that appeared in the first *sefer*. Afterwards, he instructed his *gabbai* to write *haskamos* for the *seforim*, first for the *sippurim* and then for the *chiddushim*. Reb Aizik was impressed with the *tzaddik*'s *pilpul*, on the second *sefer*, but was perplexed by the precedence he had given to the *sippurei tzaddikim*. A few days later, at a *Rosh Chodesh seuda*, the *tzaddik* suddenly spoke up, "This *gaon* is surprised at the priority I gave to the *sippurim*. In fact, this was addressed long ago by Rashi, who inquires why the *Torah* begins with the story of the *avos*, before listing the *mitzvos*. This is because the *sippurim* communicate to us about the greatness of *Hashem*'s involvement in the world." Turning to Reb Aizik, he concluded, "I followed the same order the *Torah* used."

Stories to Lift us Up

Praying Together

Once, the holy Ba'al Shem Tov was praying with a *minyan,* including some of his closest disciples. The Ba'al Shem Tov would pray at great length with intense *d'veikus,* longing and yearning for his Creator. His disciples would complete their prayers much earlier and then wait, sometimes for hours, for the *rebbe* to finish.

Once, when he extended his prayers even longer than usual, the disciples grew weary of waiting. They decided to attend to whatever they had to do, and then to gather again in the *shul* an hour later. After an hour, they had all returned, and they waited some more until the Ba'al Shem Tov had finished his prayer.

He then looked at them and accused, "You've created a great dis-unification, in that you went out to attend to your private needs and left me here alone!" Then he related to them the following parable.

It is well known that the nature of birds is to migrate to warm countries during the winter months. Once, the inhabitants of one of those countries noticed an unusually beautiful bird, with feathers of every color in the universe, and he was perched at the crest of a very high and mighty tree that was impossible to climb. When the king of the land heard about the bird, he resolved to capture it. He ordered numerous people to be brought to the forest where the tree was located. One was to stand on the shoulders of the other until they could reach the perch of the beautiful bird, and then to take it to the king.

The procedure for reaching the heights of the tree was very demanding and time consuming. Therefore, some of those at the bottom of the human ladder lost sight of the task at hand. Weary and disgruntled with the amount of time it was taking, they started to disperse. It goes without saying that the whole ladder toppled to the ground, injuring those on the highest sections. The king sought that his people should be banded together with a common purpose, but this time nothing was gained.

"It was good", concluded the Ba'al Shem Tov, "when you were bound together with me in my prayer. But when you disbanded, everyone going his own separate way, everything fell. What I had anticipated to achieve, was lost."

Faith, Just Wait

Once, the Ba'al Shem Tov was thinking about how great his faith in *Hashem* was. A heavenly voice called out, "Reb Yisroel, don't become proud. Yankel the innkeeper has more faith than you."

The Ba'al Shem Tov decided to visit Yankel the Innkeeper. He stayed there several weeks, but there didn't seem to be anything special about Yankel, until one *Shabbos*.

In the middle of the evening meal, a local peasant came in, banged three times on the table with his stick, and then left. Reb Yankel explained that it was a sign that he must soon pay the rent, 5000 rubles. Reb Yankel admitted that he didn't have the money and wasn't planning on borrowing any. *Hashem* would help, as He always had.

The next *Shabbos* the peasant returned, issuing the same warning. Reb Yankel yelled at him, "Don't come back until tomorrow." The peasant yelled back, "Jew, if you don't get the money, we are going to feed you to the dogs!"

The next day, Reb Yankel went about his business. In the morning, three businessmen came by and asked him if he could act as their agent to buy wheat for them, for the Czar, and they would pay him 2000 rubles for the effort. Yankel demanded 5000 rubles. They offered 2500, then 3000, but Yankel refused. They didn't come to an agreement, and the men left.

Around 2:00 the same afternoon, the peasant came back. He banged on the door and screamed, "Jew, pay up!"

"Get out," cried Yankel, "I have until nightfall."

A half hour before nightfall, the peasant returned. He just opened the door and walked right in. Reb Yankel was completely unperturbed. He said, "Just a minute," took his hat and walking stick and walked out to the road. At that moment, the three wheat merchants came riding over the hill. They agreed to his price, and they all went inside and closed the deal.

That, the Ba'al Shem Tov later remarked, is true faith in *Hashem*.

The Soul of the Ba'al Shem Tov

In the city of Tzfat, in *Eretz Yisroel*, once lived a simple Jew who only understood how to pray. Nevertheless, he was exceptionally modest and straightforward. One night, as he was reciting *Tikkun Chatzos*, there was a knock at the door. A man arrived and introduced himself as Eliyahu Hanavi. He came to reveal to this simple Jew the time when *moshiach* will come. But first, the man had to reveal to him what he had done on the day of his *bar-mitzvah* that earned him the privilege of receiving this information. The man declined to tell. Although it was Eliyahu HaNavi asking, what he did was completely *l'shem shamayim*, and therefore a secret between him and the Creator. Then he agreed not to receive the information.

Eliyahu HaNavi returned to heaven where there was a tremendous tumult over this man's purity. They requested Eliyahu to return and to teach this man deep secrets of *Torah*. The man developed into a great *tzaddik nistar*. When he died, the Heavenly Court decided that his reward would be to return to earth and reveal a new path in *Torah* that would renew souls, purify the world and accelerate the redemption. This was the soul of the Ba'al Shem Tov.

Hands on Work

R' Eliezer Lippa was a rather simple, but devout Jew, who dwelled in the town of Taranow in Galicia. Unlike others in the community, he was not well versed and didn't know the meaning of most of his daily prayers, but he always davened with the *minyan*. He was scrupulous to say *amen* after every blessing of the *chazan*, and to respond *amen yehey shemai rabbah*, in the *Kaddish*. He never talked about worldly matters in the *shul*, and he accorded the sages and rabbis their due honor.

He was a laborer who knew many trades, but he is best known to us as a water carrier. R' Eliezer Lippa worked hard and succeeded to make a decent living. He had four steady customers, who were well-off merchants and paid him above the average rate for his services.

Once, before he revealed himself to the world, the Ba'al Shem Tov arrived in Taranow. He appeared as a simple itinerant, but with a gift for telling stories. He used to congregate with the other laborers and tell them stories from the *Talmud*, relating to them how *Hashem* was delighted with the sincere prayers and straightforward faith of ordinary Jews.

Once, R' Eliezer Lippa was leading his wagon with its full barrel of water through the center of town when he spotted his friend, and fellow water carrier, R' Zalman Dov. He was with some other men, gathered around a ragged itinerant (the Ba'al Shem Tov) and listening intently, so as to hear his every word.

This scene sparked R' Eliezer Lippa's interest, so he went over to join the circle of listeners. The Ba'al Shem Tov was telling a story of a wealthy man, who lived in the days when the holy Temple in Jerusalem still stood.

"The wealthy man was taking a fattened ox to the Temple for a sacrifice. It was a massive beast, and when it decided, for reasons of its own, to stop still in its tracks, nobody was able to convince it to walk further towards their destination. No amount of pushing and whipping could make that animal budge.

"A poor man, who was on his way home, was watching the scene. In his hand was a bunch of freshly pulled up carrots, with the green stalks still attached to the bright orange roots. Wanting to be of help to the hapless ox owner, he held the carrots to the ox's nose, and when it began to nibble he pulled them away, thereby leading the animal to its destination at the Holy Temple.

"That night the owner of the ox had a dream. In his dream, he heard a voice calling out, 'The sacrifice of the poor man, who gave up the carrots he was bringing to his impoverished family, was a more desirable sacrifice than your fattened ox.'

"The wealthy man had brought a large fattened ox for a burnt offering. He was so joyful at being able to bring such an animal that he also brought a sheep for a peace offering and made a huge feast for his family and friends. He also distributed the proper gifts from his sacrifices to the priests. His joy was so intense that he held back nothing.

"On the other hand, the poor man in his poverty had only a few carrots to bring home for his family. What were his carrots compared to the fatted animal of the wealthy man?

"Nevertheless," remarked the Ba'al Shem Tov, "*Hashem* desires the heart. Any *mitzvah* a person may do, whether great or small, simple or difficult, is judged by how it is performed. A *mitzvah* done for *Hashem's* sake, with great *simchah* and purity of heart, is very precious to the Creator. *Hashem* cries out to the angels, 'Look at the *mitzvah* my son/daughter has done!' *Hashem* from his place in the heavens saw that although the wealthy man had offered much, the poor man had offered much more."

R' Eliezer Lippa's mind became uneasy. How he longed to be able to do a *mitzvah* like the poor man in the story, with pure intention and a joyful, overflowing heart. Many weeks passed and still R' Eliezer Lippa had no peace of mind, as the desire to do such a *mitzvah* tortured his heart.

One day, as R' Eliezer Lippa went about his normal routine of delivering water to one of his wealthy customers. He suddenly had an idea, an idea so perfect that his whole being became infused with a deep sense of pleasure and relief. R' Eliezer Lippa's four wealthy customers sustained him with half of his livelihood, since they paid him far more than the regular rate for a barrel of water. On the other hand, his friend R' Zalman Dov distributed to the town's four *shuls*, which paid him half price for their water. He thought, "I can switch four of my customers for four of his; four wealthy homes for four synagogues." He was enthusiastic to serve *Hashem* by providing the water for the congregants to wash their hands. Certainly, the *mitzvah* was of more value than the profits he would give up.

He returned home and related to his wife the story of the Ba'al Shem Tov, and how doing a *mitzvah* with joy is like bringing a sacrifice in the holy Temple (even though it no longer stands). She readily agreed to the idea, as did R' Zalman Dov who didn't mind the extra income. The deal was completed, and the transfer of customers was made. Only R' Eliezer Lippa and his wife knew what had happened and they were overjoyed at the prospects for their new "business". There were times when even R' Eliezer Lippa's wife went to the river to contribute in the *mitzvah* of "drawing water for the synagogues."

All the while, they would concentrate on the *mitzvah* of preparing water for the congregants to wash their hands before prayers, and their joy was boundless for they understood that *Hashem* desires the heart.

According to some, the story didn't end here. In the *zechus*, merit of the *mitzvah* which R' Eliezer Lippa and his wife performed they were blessed with children, for she had formerly been barren. Those children matured to be luminaries who lit up the Jewish world and inspired tens of thousands of Jews to return to *Hashem* in *teshuvah*, serving *Hashem* with joy.

Those sons were R' Elimelech of Lizhenzsk and R' Zusha of Anipoli, two of the primary students of the Ba'al Shem Tov's successor, the Maggid of Mezeritch.

Teshuvah Before He Left the World

There was once a *chassid* from a neighboring town who came to Reb Hirsh Riminover. He began begging him to somehow intercede so that his father-in-law would die. "What!" exclaimed Reb Hirsh, "What are you talking about?"

"Well, my father-in-law is very old, already more than 100 years." clarified the *chassid*, "and he has to be watched over constantly. He can't really do much for himself, and he is miserable most of the time. He doesn't learn and doesn't *daven* any more. He has had enough of life already, but he just keeps hanging on day after day, week after week, year after year."

R' Hirsh was bewildered and didn't really know what to say. He reasoned that a *Yid* who lived to such an age must have merit. He commanded the *chassid* to bring in the old man to him so that he could speak with him. The *chassid* objected that his father was too old and too fragile, but R' Hirsh wouldn't relent. "Bring him in anyway as I have requested," he ordered.

So, he did as he was told and picked up the old man, bringing him to Riminov. He carried him in on a bed and positioned him in front of R' Hirsh. R' Hirsh commenced to ask him questions, and soon discovered that the old man had been a simple, boorish Jew. He had been a wagon driver, the entirety of his life. He *davened* in the morning, but his actual interest was to get to breakfast and eat. He went to *shul* on *Shabbos*, but the *cholent* was his objective.

R' Hirsh badgered him with more questions to find out if the old Jew could remember any reason that might shed light on his many years. He understood that there was something behind this story, and he wasn't going to give up until he found out what it was. Maybe there was some special *mitzvah* that he did once that he might not remember. Maybe he had been to a *tzaddik* on some special occasion and received a *brachah* for a long life.

Then the old *Yiddalah* recollected that once some *avrechim* had asked him to take them for *Shabbos* to a town about a half a day's journey away called Lizhenzsk. "They pleaded with me, but I had no interest in going. I explained to them how I like *Shabbos* at home with my bed and my *cholent.* They persisted, and they promised me a good wage, and the same food that I would eat at home, with extras to boot. So, I was unable to refuse, and we set off. We arrived there, not long before *Shabbos,* and they put me up in a pleasant hotel.

"Sure enough, right after the *davening,* they showed up with a great meal, everything, just as I like it. They came back a little while later, and they asked me if I wanted to go with them to some kind of gathering. I told them that I didn't come for that kind of thing, and they should let me sleep. So, being decent guys, they did.

"In the morning after the *davening,* they again brought me a satisfying meal, with a cholent even better than what I would have gotten at home. I ate my fill and went to sleep.

"When I got up from my nap it was close to dark, and nobody was around. I waited awhile but none of my passengers showed their faces. So, I went to look for them. I came to the *shul,* and I heard the loudest singing and wildest dancing you can imagine. It sounded like they were all *shikkur.* I peeked inside and there were empty bottles on the table, and these guys were singing and dancing like anything. When I went in I saw that they were in a circle and they were all dancing around with one of them in the middle. He must have been the chief *shikkur,* or something, because he was tall, and his face was red like fire. He was dancing with his eyes closed and they were all singing and dancing around him."

At this stage, R' Hirsh stopped the old man, exclaiming that now he understood the whole shebang. The tall one in the middle whose face shone like red fire was none other than R' Elimelech of Lizhenzsk. He said it was well known that anybody who ever saw, or even just glimpsed the face of R' Elimelech, would not be able to leave the world until he had done complete *teshuvah.*

Afterwards, R' Hirsh turned towards the old gentleman and started to explain to him in a soft fatherly tone how *Hashem* created the world, and how everything in it was put there for our benefit. He went on to describe the beauty of the creation, and how every aspect of it is perfect, existing together in total harmony.

Then he commenced to explain the nature of the precious Jewish soul. He went on to describe how every Jew is like one *neshamah.* We are only separated by our physical bodies. Afterwards, he gave us the *Torah* and its *mitzvos*, specific instructions for serving *Hashem* and understanding His will.

The old Jew sat and listened but did not utter a word.

So, R' Hirsh continued to teach. He commenced to describe how we were given the *Shabbos* to further bring ourselves closer to *Hashem*. We embrace the *Shabbos, and Hashem* comes to us to set His presence at our table, sharing our food and company.

At this point, the old *Yiddalah* turned his head and stared dreamily outside the window. A few moments passed, and he let out a deep sigh. R' Hirsh (who was a *Kohen*) hurriedly ordered all of the *Kohanim* to immediately leave the room (*Kohanim* even today are forbidden contact with the dead). The old Jew heaved one more sigh of remorseful repentance and departed this world for the next world.

Our Logic Isn't His

R' Zusha of Anipoli yet again found himself in debt with the repayment date arriving the next morning, and the resources with which to repay nowhere in sight.

R' Zusha however, was a *tzaddik* with perfect faith. Long ago, he had consigned himself totally in the hands of the Creator of the world, and he had no need to be concerned.

So, R' Zusha, aspiring to further demonstrate to his Creator how perfect his faith and trust were, sat down with a piece of paper. Thereon he recorded 25 different scenarios in which the money needed to pay back the debt could come his way. The rest of the evening commenced, and R' Zusha gave the situation no further thought.

The morning arrived, and no sooner did R' Zusha conclude his morning prayers than the required sum manifested itself before him. But the money arrived in R' Zusha's hand in a 26th way, according to a scenario that he hadn't thought to record.

"Oy yoy, oy yoy," he moaned, thoroughly disappointed with himself for the whole episode. "Is the Creator of the World limited to the feeble ideas of R' Zusha?"

Hashem Brings Me Food

It was the custom of R' Zusha of Anipoli to recite his morning prayers for a long time. When he finished, he would retire to his room next to the *shul*. He would then open the window in his room, lifting his eyes to the heavens while calling out, "Master of the World, Zusha (he commonly referred to himself in the third person) is very hungry and desires to eat something!"

Each morning, his attendant would wait till he heard R' Zusha's appeal, then he would bring in R' Zusha's morning meal of cake with a little schnapps.

One time, the attendant thought to himself, "Why doesn't R' Zusha request me directly for his meal? In fact, who does he think he is fooling by calling out to *Hashem* in that way? He knows full well that I bring him his food each day." So, he thereby decided that the following morning he would not bring R' Zusha's meal when he called out. Rather, he would just wait it out and see what would happen. Where would R' Zusha look for his meal?

The next day R' Zusha awoke as usual, well before the light of day commenced. He followed his regular morning routine. First, he went to the town *mikvah* to immerse himself in preparation for the day's holy *avodah*. The past night had been a rainy one in Anipoli, and the streets of the town had now turned to rivers of mud. In order to progress from one side of the street to another, one had to traverse on narrow planks that were laid across the flowing mud. As R' Zusha was journeying in the direction of the *mikvah*, a man whom he didn't recognize, a stranger in town, was coming towards R' Zusha from the other side. When he spotted R' Zusha, gaunt, nearly emaciated, dressed in rags without barely a tooth in his mouth, the stranger yelled out, "Itinerant!" Then with a hearty laugh he jumped up and down on the plank, causing R' Zusha to flip into the mud.

R' Zusha lay speechless. He calmly picked himself out of the mud and restarted his way to the *mikvah*. All the while, the stranger sauntered off into the distance, snickering merrily while he re-enacted his great prank over and over in his mind. Arriving back at the inn where he was lodging, he couldn't resist bragging to the innkeeper about his prank. The innkeeper didn't react the same way. He questioned the guest to depict the "itinerant" whom he had catapulted into the mud. He suddenly put his hands to his head and cried out in anguish, *"Oy VaVoy, Oy Oy,* do you know what you did!? That was not just some itinerant, that was the holy R' Zusha!"

Now it was the turn of the guest to cry out *"Oy VaVoy"*. R' Zusha was known to all as a holy man and a *tzaddik*. Trembling, the guest cried out, *"Oy Vey, Oy Vey!* What am I going to do now? What am I going to do now?"

"Don't worry" exclaimed the innkeeper, recomposing himself. "Listen to me. I know what you should do. R' Zusha spends countless hours every morning in prayer. When he finishes, he heads into his private room next to the *shul*. There he unfastens the window, and everybody can see how he leans out and lifting his eyes to heaven calls out, 'Master of the world, Zusha is very hungry and desires to eat something!' So, let me prepare some cakes and some schnapps for you to bring him. Then, after you hear him call out to the Creator, you go in immediately with this gift, and offer it to him while begging for his forgiveness. I'm certain that he will then forgive you whole-heartedly."

That day, like every morning following the prayers, R' Zusha headed to his room, opened the window and exclaimed, "Master of the world, Zusha is very hungry and desires to eat something!" Meanwhile, the attendant, upon hearing R' Zusha, held his ground, waiting to see what the outcome would be. "Let *Hashem* bring him his cake this morning," he huffed to himself.

Suddenly, the door to the *shul* opened and a man holding a large plate of cakes and a bottle of schnapps entered, making his way to the room of R' Zusha. He went without delay, put the cakes on the table, and then plunged to the floor in grief, begging the *tzaddik* for his forgiveness (which was certainly granted).

Now it was clear to the attendant that it really was the Master of the world who brought R' Zusha his breakfast every morning. He was only a simple messenger.

A Ready Mikvah

Rabbi Yisrael Rubin, *shaliach* in Albany, NY, related the following tale:

"One day I received an unexpected directive from the late Rebbe of Chabad to build a mikvah in the town of Troy. We were very amazed by this instruction because Troy was a remote place with only a few elderly Jews living there, and it was highly unlikely that there would ever be a Jewish community there. This instruction therefore seemed very strange.

"Two years later, the state authorities decided to open a computer city, rather like a Silicon Valley, and of all the places in New York, they chose Troy as its location.

"Many of the young people working in computers today are Jewish, and within a short while, many young Jewish families had settled in Troy.

"The *mikvah* was already built for them, and it didn't take long for us to bring a *shaliach* to the town."

Tick Tock

Once the *chassidic* master, Reb Dov Ber of Radoshitz, was traveling through the Polish countryside. Nightfall arrived and the roads would soon be unsafe. So, he directed his wagon driver to stop at the first Jewish inn they came upon.

Soon they pulled up in front of a small Jewish tavern. The owner welcomed them, assisted them with their bags, and fed and watered their horse. He then prepared for Reb Dov Ber a special room for traveling rabbis and noblemen. After praying the evening prayer, Reb Dov Ber retired to bed, tired after the long day's journey.

Soon the tavern became quiet and the fields outside became still. Only the occasional barking of a lone farm dog could be heard in the silence of the night. Yet, Reb Dov Ber was tossing and turning in his bed. It was the clock on the wall disturbing him -- it was ticking in the most amazing way, it wouldn't let him sleep. He arose and began pacing the room. Verses from the books of the prophets filled his mind, along with songs of deliverance and hope. He tried again to lie down, but the clock kept ticking, until he had no choice but to rise from bed again. Thus, he spent the night, pacing the room in anxious anticipation. It was clear he wasn't going to get any sleep.

In the morning, as much as he was tired, he also felt exhilarated. The *rabbi* approached the innkeeper. "Where did you get that clock in the room?"

The innkeeper responded, "That clock? Well, some years ago, another rabbi lodged in the room, Reb Yosef of Turchin, the son of that *tzaddik*, the Seer of Lublin. He came for just one night, but the weather spoiled, and he was forced to remain for several days. When he concluded his stay, he found that he did not have enough funds to pay the bill, so he covered the difference by offering me that clock. He said that he had inherited it from his father."

"Now I understand why I couldn't sleep," related Reb Dov Ber. "Most clocks in the world only cause depression, for they count the hours that have passed - another day lost, another opportunity gone by. But the clock of the holy Seer of Lublin counts the time that is coming - another minute closer to the final redemption, another second to the age of universal peace."

Wherever is Your Mind

Rebbe Levi Yitzchok of Berditchev strolled over to one of the congregants and extended his hand. The man had just completed saying the *Amidah* prayer, and Rebbe Levi Yitzchok greeted him with a hearty *shalom aleichem.*

"*Rebbe,*" the man questioned, "why are you greeting me as if I returned form a journey? I live here in Berditchev, and we see each other often. I haven't traveled outside the city for quite some time."

"I watched you while you were praying," responded the *rebbe.* "As you narrated your prayers, you were planning your next voyage to the commercial fair in Leipzig. You visualized your transactions so powerfully that you felt as if you had traveled to and from the fair already. After such a journey, I felt it only proper that I should greet you cordially."

I love You, Hashem

The Ba'al Shem Tov on one occasion invited his students, "Come, let us go learn a lesson in the love of *Hashem.*"

He escorted them to a nearby open field where a shepherd tended his flock. Spontaneously, the shepherd elevated his voice towards heaven and exclaimed: "Dear *Hashem*, I love you so! I will dance for You to show You my great love."

With that, the simple shepherd broke into a joyful dance. After finishing his dance, he turned yet again towards the heavens. "Dear *Hashem*, my love for You has no bounds! I will express my love by jumping back and forth across this small pond."

After jumping back and forth for while, he called heavenward once more: "What can I offer You to prove my deep love for You, Oh *Hashem*! Here, I have a coin in my pocket- I will give it to You." The shepherd took the coin and cast it heavenward. [Some versions of the story relate that the coin did not descend.]

Only Happy Words

Rav Hillel of Paritch never recited *al naharos Bavel* (Psalm 137) before he would recite the grace after eating. He always sought a reason to recite *shir hama'alos* (Psalm 126) instead. He did so during the weekdays, and even when there was no apparent reason.

A Tzaddik's prayer

Numerous *chassidim* were peering into the Tzemach Tzedek's study, through a crack in the door. They were inquiring as to why the *rebbe* chose to lock himself in his room instead of joining the evening service as usual. The secretive *chassidim* saw that he had drawn a circle around himself and was praying in deep concentration. Why, they had no idea.

The *chassidim* at the door recoiled in awe at the sound of his heartbreaking cries to *Hashem*. Suddenly, the Tzemach Tzedek pronounced the words, "He who saves us from the hands of Kings." He then stepped out of the circle and resumed his usual manner of prayer.

Several days later, word of the evil Czar Nikolai's death arrived in Lubavitch.

Just One Spoonful

A Jewish home always has a hot bowl of meat waiting for its festive *Shabbos* meals. The steaming-hot cholent had been served at Rabbi Hillel of Paritch's *Shabbos* table. One of the guests courteously declined his portion, excusing himself by explaining, "My doctor has forbidden me to eat this heavy food."

"Just have a taste." Rabbi Hillel impelled him. "I take full responsibility for your well-being."

The guest helped himself to one spoonful. Its taste was very alluring, and he wanted to scoop up another spoon. Rabbi Hillel, however, cautioned him: "Any more is your own responsibility."

The Rhizhiner's Tefillin

The Rizhiner Rebbe, Rabbi Yisroel of Rizhin, was the great-grandson of the Maggid of Mezritch.

The Rizhiner Rebbe had inherited his great-grandfather's *tefillin*, and when the Rizhiner Rebbe left this world, his six sons all wanted this most prized possession. The brothers resolved to cast lots, and David Moshe was the winner.

Many years passed. Rabbi Avraham Yaakov, the eldest son of the Rizhiner Rebbe, was now renowned as the *rebbe* of Sadigura. Once, the Sadigura Rebbe revealed to his *chassidim* that he had wanted to have the special *tefillin* inherited by his brother, Rabbi David Moshe.

A young *chassid* exposed in a trembling voice, "Knowing how much the *rebbe* had wanted the *Maggid's tefillin*, my friend and I traveled to Rabbi David Moshe's home and secretly took the parchments out of the *tefillin* boxes, replacing them with perfectly *kosher* parchments. We meant no harm to the *rebbe's* brother and only hoped to please the *rebbe*. Afterwards, we had second thoughts but now that we heard how much the *rebbe* had wanted the *Maggid's tefillin*, we have decided to tell the *rebbe* what we did."

The *chassidim* who overheard this confession shivered in disbelief. How could they do such a dreadful thing? On the other hand, they thought, if Rabbi David Moshe stayed unaware, then perhaps the *tefillin* really weren't intended for him?

The Sadigura Rebbe unwrapped the parchments, glanced over them carefully, lovingly rewrapped them in his silk kerchief and put them aside. "We will go visit my brother," spoke the *rebbe*.

Once the Sadigura Rebbe and his *chassidim* reached the town of Potick, his brother welcomed them graciously. The next morning, Rabbi David Moshe ushered his brother into a private room where they were to pray together. On the desk lay three pairs of *tefillin* next to each other - Rashi, Rabbeinu Tam, and *Shimushah Rabbah*. A little beyond them was another pair of *tefillin* in a bag that the Sadigura Rebbe acknowledged as the *Maggid's tefillin*.

Rabbi David Moshe embraced the *Maggid's tefillin* with his eyes closed in contemplation. Then he sighed and placed them back down. He then put on his own Rashi *tefillin* and started to pray. Afterwards, he put on the other two pairs of *tefillin*.

When they concluded praying, the Sadigura Rebbe asked his brother why he did not wear the saintly *Maggid's tefillin*. Rabbi David Moshe sighed once more. "I have not put them on, since, one morning when I picked them up and did not feel their holiness. This could only mean that I am no longer worthy to put them on." Rabbi David Moshe went on, saying to his brother, "I want you to have these *tefillin*. I am sure that you are worthier than I."

The Sadigura Rebbe commented, "These *tefillin* truly are meant for you." And he proceeded to tell his brother what had transpired. Upon finishing, the Sadigura Rebbe took out his silk kerchief and gave it to his brother. "I am sure that as soon as you replace these in their boxes, you will once again feel their holiness."

Soon after that, Rabbi David Moshe moved to Tchortkow and became well-known as the Tchortkower Rebbe. When he felt that his soul would return to his Maker, he said to his only son, Yisrael, "I am leaving the *Maggid's tefillin* to you, as an inheritance. Cherish them and guard them well," he told him.

Rabbi Yisrael wore the *Maggid's tefillin* only twice each year, during *Purim* and on the eve of *Yom Kippur*. On all other days, he used his own *tefillin*. During World War I, Rabbi Yisrael and his family had to vacate their home in Tchortkow in great haste. During the sudden rush, the *tefillin* were forgotten behind. Rabbi Yisrael was heartbroken, but it was out of his hands at this point. It wasn't safe to return to get them. He and his family found temporary refuge in Lvov. When the Russians then threatened Lvov, they relocated to Vienna till the conclusion of the war. Some years later, the Russians were driven out of Galicia and Tchortkow was finally liberated. Although he tried, Rabbi Yisrael was not able to return to Tchortkow to search for the *Maggid's tefillin*.

Sometime after the war, Rabbi Yisrael was visited by a Jewish prisoner of war. Surprisingly, the soldier took out a *tefillin* bag from his rucksack and gave it to Rabbi Yisrael. The *rebbe* kissed the *tefillin*. In a trembling voice, he remarked, "I always knew that somehow these *tefillin* would make their way back to me. You have completed the great *mitzvah* of returning a lost item. Where did you get these?"

The soldier commenced to tell how he ended up finding the *tefillin*. "I was serving in the Russian army. When we were chasing the Austrians, we reached Tchortkow. I had been to Tchortkow as a child; my father was a *chassid* of the *rebbe*. I recognized the *rebbe's* house, and I saw soldiers ransacking it. I went inside because I could feel that one room was permeated with holiness. I searched in the debris and found this *tefillin* bag!"

Continuing the story, the soldier confessed, "I survived the war due to many miracles, which I attribute to the fact that the *tefillin* were in my possession. I was captured and became a prisoner of war. I was recently released and am now on my way home. My first stop was to find the *rebbe* and bring him his *tefillin*."

"*Hashem* will surely reward you for your great *mitzvah* and for the immense pleasure that you have brought me. I insist that you be my guest for a few days. Please wait a moment while I go ask my attendant to make the arrangements."

The *rebbe* talked with his attendant and then returned to his room, but the soldier was nowhere to be seen. The *rebbe* called in his attendant and instructed him, "Quickly, bring the soldier back who just left my room!"

"I did not see anyone leave the *rebbe's* room," the attendant answered. Was this really a soldier that returned the *tefillin* or was it Eliyahu Hanavi?

Tefillin Letters Reappear

R. Dovid of Stefin, a simple *talmid* of the *Maggid*, somehow managed to acquire a choice pair of *tefillin*. He once discovered something incorrect with a letter in one of the *parshios*, and brought it to the *Maggid*. The *Maggid* took the *parshah*, positioned it upon his own brow, and the letter was repaired.

"But shouldn't the letters of the *tefillin* be written in order?" inquired R. Dovid. "And therefore, are they not still *pasul*?"

The *Maggid* responded, "Originally, there was nothing wrong with these *tefillin*. However, someone who *davened* with them improperly caused a 'barrier' to form over the letter. Once I sanctified it upon my forehead, the barrier dissolved, and the letter reappeared as before. Therefore, the *tefillin* are now *kosher*."

Both North and South

A wealthy *misnagid*, fascinated by *chassidus*, became a *talmid* of the *Maggid*, and soon lost his riches. He questioned the *Maggid*, "Why did I become poor after I began following you?"

"Our sages have taught, 'Whoever seeks wisdom should go south, and whoever seeks wealth should head north.' It's impossible to be in two places at once," the *Maggid* remarked.

"So, nothing can be done?" the man persisted.

"There is one way," replied the *Maggid*. "One who diminishes himself and becomes as naught, and takes up no space, can thus go both north and south."

Just Believe in Hashem

A villager and his wife went to the *Maggid*, looking to be blessed with a son. The *Maggid* suggested fifty-two rubles for his efforts, fifty-two being the *gematria* of the word *ben*. The villager only had twenty-one rubles; however, R. Dov Ber refused them.

Desperate, the villager collected more money, and placed it before the *Maggid*. Still R. Dov Ber insisted that it still wasn't enough.

"Let's take the money back," the villager suggested to his wife. "*Hashem* will help us without the *Maggid*."

"That's just what I was hoping to hear," exclaimed the *Maggid*. "You should trust only in *Hashem*." Within that year, they were blessed with a baby boy.

A Doctor's Angel

Passing through Mezritch on a business trip, a notable Jew from Vilna, who had heard wonderful things about the *Maggid*, decided to see for himself what the *rebbe* was all about, expecting to hear words of *Torah* from the *Maggid*. However, R. Dov Ber simply informed him, "Medicines do not always cure a person. Sometimes the mere presence of a doctor can heal, for each physician is accompanied by a Heavenly healing force, and the best are escorted by Raphael [the angel of healing] himself."

The now puzzled man dismissed these words as pointless and resumed his business.

Having returned home to Vilna, he took ill. The doctors were helpless, and his situation worsened. He lost his voice, and his family started to lose hope.

Meanwhile, a German Jew named Dr. Aharon Gordia had quit Judaism to become the personal physician to the king of Prussia and his ministers. He chanced to be in Vilna, and the family of the sick Jew sought him out.

When Dr. Gordia arrived at the Jew's home and perceived that the man's life was ebbing away, he grew angry. "I am only a doctor," he exclaimed. "I cannot resurrect the dead!" Saddened, the family members apologized to him as he set to leave. As he was departing, he noticed that the patient's face showed signs of improvement. "There's still hope", he announced as he checked the man's pulse.

Dr. Gordia sent a messenger for some medicine, but before the envoy returned he noticed that the patient had improved further, so he requested a weaker remedy. This happened numerous times, until the Jew regained consciousness.

"Doctor, please - just sit next to me," he requested. "A *rebbe* expressed to me that if a great doctor comes to see a patient, the angel Raphael himself comes with him, and a sick individual can be cured even without any medicines. Seeing that you're here and I've revived, I am persuaded that the *rebbe* was right. So please remain with me until I recover."

Astounded, Dr. Gordia wrote down the *rebbe's* name and address, provided the patient some medicine, and eventually left. He remained deeply impressed with everything he'd heard about the *Maggid,* and a long-extinguished spark of Jewishness was rekindled within him. He recalled how in his youth, in his parent's home, they had celebrated the Jewish festivals, and he developed a thirst to return to his faith.

Dr. Gordia visited Mezritch in a magnificent carriage and prepared himself to meet the *Maggid* by resolving to change his indulgent lifestyle.

"I've waited a long time for you," divulged the *Maggid* upon greeting him. "Now, I will heal your soul, and you will heal my body."

Over the following months, Dr. Gordia purified his soul and learned a great deal of *Torah*, becoming a *tzaddik* and a devotee of the *Maggid.*

Laughter Reverses Decrees

There was once a sickly man who suffered great pain. He decided to visit the *Maggid* for a *brachah*, giving him a *pidyon.* To the astonishment of R. Elimelech of Lizhenzsk, R. Dov Ber burst out laughing. "Laughter creates joy," he insisted, "which is rooted in *chachmah*, which contains the ability to correct an abnormality. That is why I laughed, to alter the stern decree imposed on him."

Learn From a Baby

The *Maggid* said, "There are three things you can learn from a baby. A baby is always happy, and never depressed. He is never idle, even for a moment. And when he needs something from his father, even something insignificant, he immediately cries out."

Dancing Before Eliyahu

Traveling to the wedding in Chernobyl, R. Shlomo and R. Shalom Shachna went through Berditchev and R. Levi Yitzchak honored them with a festive meal.

As they departed Berditchev, R. Levi Yitzchak sent musicians to escort them out of town while he personally danced before them. Later, his wife asked, "Why did you have to lower yourself by dancing like a child? Wasn't it enough that you treated them to such a banquet?"

"How could I not dance before the groom," retorted R. Levi Yitzchak, "when Eliyahu Hanavi was dancing, too?"

Don't Overeat

Notwithstanding his royal demeanor, R. Shalom Shachna ate as little as his father and relished very little of the wealth with which he surrounded himself. "One should always eat and drink sparingly," he contended. "A camel hardly eats but lives long, while a horse eats a lot and his days are few."

Happy for Abba

On *erev Succos*, 1802, R. Shalom Shachna left this world, at the age of forty-two. His oldest son, R. Avraham, then just sixteen, arrived in the *succah* and sat in his father's chair, his face full of joy.

"Why are you happy?" his mother insisted. "No one rejoices after his father's death!"

"Mother," R. Avraham rejoined immediately, "if you were to see our father's exalted state in Heaven, you would be as ecstatic as I."

It Was Not I

One evening, R. Shneur Zalman of Liadi knocked on the *Maggid's* door. "Who's there?" enquired the *Maggid*.

"It is I," remarked R. Shneur Zalman.

"Who?" R. Dov Ber repeated.

"It is I," R. Shneur Zalman replied.

"Who?" the *Maggid* asked again.

"Shneur Zalman," he answered. With that, he was ultimately admitted.

At the *Maggid's* request, the following day R. Shneur Zalman went to a *bris milah* held in a neighboring village. Noticing R. Shneur Zalman's old and tattered clothing, it was assumed that he was a beggar, and he was seated at the end of the table.

Whilst sitting there, a silver spoon was found missing after the *seudah*. The "beggar" being an easy mark, was immediately suspected of theft. Denying the charge, he bellowed, "It was not I!" His opponents began to beat him. "It was not I," he kept repeating.

Eventually, it was exposed that an attendant had taken the spoon, and R. Shneur Zalman was exonerated. Returing to Mezritch, the *Maggid* was awaiting him.

"How many times did you have to shout, 'Not I?'" he questioned his astounded student.

"Two times you announced to me, 'It is I'. There is only One in the universe who may say this. If we are mindful of *Hashem's* presence, how can we, mere mortals, conceit ourselves on being 'I'? We must strive for total *bittul*, self-effacement.

"Twice you called yourself 'I,' so two times you required to announce, 'It is not I.'"

I am Absolutely Nothing

"So, what did you learn while in Mezritch from your *rebbe*, the *Maggid?*" R. Aharon of Karlin was questioned.

"Absolutely nothing!" he retorted.

"What do you mean?" cried his questioners.

"I learned that I am absolutely nothing!"

The Mouth of the Shechinah

R. Zev of Zhitomir wrote of his experience with the *Maggid*, "Many times I saw with my own eyes that when he opened his mouth to speak words of *Torah*, he appeared as if he were not in this world at all, rather as if the *Shechinah* were speaking through him."

Fainted at the Sight

"Once on *Rosh Hashanah*, during *Minchah*, I saw the *Maggid's* face, as resplendent as a beautiful rainbow," revealed R. Levi Yitzchak. "Filled with fear and trembling, I fell backwards. People supported me, unable to understand why I had fallen. When my master saw my trembling, he turned to the wall and I saw no more."

Daven with a Torn Heart

R. Azriel and R. Yisrael of Politzk once resolved to search for a *rebbe's* guidance. That night while dreaming, R. Yisrael imagined an image of a righteous man and was told that this *tzaddik* would "open their hearts". The two embarked immediately to find him.

Following years of wandering, they chanced upon the *Maggid's* house, where R. Yisrael recognized the *Maggid's* face from his dream.

When he returned to Politzk, R. Azriel was questioned by his comrades what he had learned at the *Maggid's*. "The *Maggid*," he answered, "taught me that one must *daven* with a seething, torn heart, as if a cruel armed bandit were about to slay him!"

Genius in Everything

As in Medzibozh, not every lesson in Mezritch was taught using conventional methods. However, one found holiness and Divine genius in everything. Every movement spoke volumes. As R. Leib Sarah's told over, "I traveled to the *Maggid* not to hear *Torah* from him, but to see how he ties and unties his shoelaces."

Let Him Enter First

The Jews of two, towns Frankfurt and Nikolsburg, requested both R. Pinchas and R. Shmelke to serve as their rabbis, leaving the brothers to resolve who would become the *rabbi* of Frankfurt, the more prestigious position, and which of them would become the rabbi of Nikolsburg. It was a very tough decision. Granting R. Shmelke was older, he felt that R. Pinchas was more suitable for Frankfurt. They conclusively decided to consult the *Maggid*, and to use their visit to receive his elucidation of an unfathomable passage in the *Zohar* as well.

Having arrived in Mezritch, each maintained that the other was greater and should therefore see the *Maggid* first.

"The rabbi of Nikolsburg should come in first, for he is older," the *Maggid* declared, thus affording the brothers the answer to their problem.

When they approached him, he articulated to them a story of a high-ranking minister, and of how he handled his servants and mansions. Having finished the story, he bid them farewell before they could ask about the *Zohar*. Later they grasped that the story had been a parable through which they could understand the enigmatic *Zohar*.

Let the Torah Master You

When R. Shneur Zalman once visited Berditchev, long after the passing of the Ba'al Shem Tov. All of the scholars there marveled at his *Torah* brilliance. "Mine is nothing compared to that of my master, the *Maggid*, and his son, the *Malach*. And both followed in the footsteps of the holy Ba'al Shem Tov, whose genius was incomparable," he remarked.

What else did the author of the *Tanya* gain from the *Maggid*? "Elsewhere one learns how to master the *Torah*. In Mezritch, one learns to let the *Torah* master you."

There is None Like Our G-d

R. Yaakov Yitzchak of Lublin, later identified as the Chozeh (Seer) of Lublin, first came to the *Maggid* while in his youth. The *Maggid* used to *daven* unaccompanied each morning, and only towards the end of his prayers would he summon nine of his finest students to form a *minyan*. R. Yaakov Yitzchak once attempted to be among the privileged nine, but the instructor requested someone else, branding him a *batlan*. When they were unable to find anyone else, though, he remained to complete the minyan.

As the *Maggid* commenced to recite *Ein K'Elokeinu* (There is None like Our G-d), R. Yaakov Yitzchak fainted, and was revived only with extreme difficulty.

"Didn't I tell you not to allow that young man in?" the *Maggid* retorted. "When I recited *Ein K'Elokeinu*, he saw the Heavenly host and instantaneously became frightened and fainted. Someone with eyes of flesh wouldn't have seen anything at all."

"At that moment," recalled the *Chozeh*, "all seven firmaments opened before my eyes, and I saw clearly that 'there is none like our God.'"

A Teacher's Sacrifice

The Ba'al Shem Tov said, "A preacher is like a broom that becomes dirty as it cleans. Similarly, one who wishes to purify hearts with his *mussar* must fall somewhat from his level, for his flock's strange thoughts, fall upon him.

Charity Before the End of the Night

When speaking about trusting in *Hashem* and believing that He will give us everything we need, the *rebbe* mentioned an exceptionally special custom of the Ba'al Shem Tov. The *rebbe's* great-grandfather would never leave any money in his possession overnight. Rather before each day was over, he would make sure to distribute all he had to charity.

There are No Wicked Jews

Reb Dovid of Lelov and Reb Yitzchok of Vorki were once lodging in a small village and resolved to visit the Jewish families there. When they reached the house of a certain unscrupulous, public sinner, Reb Yitzchok tried to prevent Reb Dovid from entering. "*Rebbe*," he explained to him, "That man is truly wicked!" Reb Dovid paid no heed and pointed to the *mezuzah* on the door. "How can you say he is wicked? See, he has a *mezuzah*."

In the Torah, We Will Be Safe

During the outbreak of World War I, the Germans conquered Lithuania from the Russians. The course of Elye Zvi's life was changed by trials of the war, and he began to move outside the confines of Kelm. On the very same day that the Germans approached Kelm and the Russians made ready to bar their progress, fighting broke out in the town itself and shells fell, wounding some of the inhabitants. Most of its inhabitants had fled by cart or on foot, some to faraway places and others to neighboring villages. However, Reb Elye began to say his customary shiur to his students. As the fighting drew closer to the center of the town, he concentrated his students' attention, with encouragement and mussar. He related the story of Rabbi Akiva and Pappos. When they were in such a dangerous situation they said, "If we are in danger in the place which is our natural habitat, i.e. beside the *gemarah* – how much more will we endanger our lives if we leave it." However, not all the students were captivated by his words. When one inquisitive student leaned his head out of the window to see what was happening in the town, he was wounded in the face by a revolver shot. Maintaining superb courage, he persisted with the students, most from other towns, and they did not leave the place until the fighting had passed. Thus, he remained at his post in Kelm after its conquest. (*Sefer Lev Eliyahu* intro p. 11)

Frozen in Prayer

I once traveled on a fast day to the Chevron *yeshivah,* where it was normal to say *Minchah* soon after midday. I saw Reb Elye standing, holding a *gemarah,* his face sparkling. I turned to one of those near to him and he related to me that he had been standing learning in the same posture, without movement, since immediately after the morning service. (*Sefer Lev Eliyahu* intro p. 27)

I Have to Learn Mussar First

It was Reb Elye Zvi's custom to recite a weekly *mussar* lesson in the *yeshivah.* On one occasion, he was out of town and returned approximately an hour before the customary time for his talk. I enquired of him if he intended to give his usual class and the answer was "no". I then remarked, "I suppose you are fatigued after your journey?" But he replied, "That is not the reason. I never speak to others unless I am gripped by the topic. In consequence, I always learn *mussar* for two hours before speaking. Since there is just one hour left before the time of my talk I cannot undertake to speak." (*Sefer Lev Eliyhu* intro)

Standing, Non-Stop Learning

Reb Elye related that it was his habit as a *bochur* to learn *Torah* standing on his feet for six hours on end during the third session of study. He also used to learn without pause from Thursday morning, during the whole of Thursday night, and Friday until just before the beginning of the *Shabbos.* After his marriage, he departed from his wife and studied in *yeshiva* in Kelm, returning only for the festivals. At that time, he learned with the outstanding scholars of that generation and went through the whole *Shulchan Aruch* with the commentary of the Gaon of Vilna. (*Sefer Lev Eliyhu* intro p. 30)

The Best Blessing

Whenever Reb Elye was asked for a blessing, it was his routine to reply, "I bless you that *Hashem* shall bless you. That is the best possible blessing." (Sefer Lev Eliyhu intro p. 31)

The Amen Miracle

A student was once traveling by train with Reb Elye from Jerusalem to Haifa and asked him if it was necessary to recite the prayer for going on a journey. He replied in amazement, "Of course it is necessary." After a while Reb Elye went to the restroom. When he left, and washed his hands, he beckoned a guard who stood near. He requested of him to summon all the guards, of whom quite a number were in his coach. When they had gathered round him he turned to them and said, "I am about to say the blessing, *Asher Yatzar*, after relieving myself and want you all to say '*amen*'." One of the guards later remarked that just listening to Reb Elye's blessing one could be moved to repentance. A few minutes later the train stopped and remained standing for about half an hour. It later became known that a bomb had been found beneath the rails and it was a miracle that it had not exploded. Reb Elye went on learning as usual. When the clamor of talk grew louder, and people spoke about what had happened, Reb Elye asked the student what the noise was about. On being told, he said to him: "What do you say now? Is it necessary to recite the prayer for a journey?" (*Sefer Lev Eliyhu* intro page 41)

It seems quite clear that both blessings of Reb Elye saved the train. We should never underestimate the importance of saying our blessings out loud so that others can recite amen.

A Marked Piece of Fish

Reb Yaakov Yitzchak paid a visit to Mezeritch for the first time. He was still a very young man at the time, not yet renowned as the Chozeh of Lublin, and his intention was to study *Torah* at the feet of Reb Dov Ber, the Maggid of Mezeritch.

As soon as he reached his destination, on a Friday afternoon, he proceeded straight into the kitchen and told those who were busy cooking the *Shabbos* meals, "I am accustomed to personally taking some part in the preparation of the fish that I am to eat on *Shabbos*. With your permission, I would like to maintain that custom today too."

He then took up a portion of fish, salted it, put it down, and went his way.

The disciples of the *Maggid* who had observed this little incident were somewhat surprised, and asked each other: "What makes this young man think that precisely this piece of fish is going to be served to him? Obviously, it will be mixed up among all the other pieces. They are all being cooked together, and it will all be divided up and served by the waiters to the various people who will be sitting at the *rebbe's* table!"

As such, they dismissed the callow newcomer's action as bizarre, or worse, pretentious.

Now, one of the cleverer disciples was a young man known affectionately by his colleagues as Zalmanyu—the same who was destined to become famous as Reb Schneur Zalman of Liadi, the author of *Tanya*. This youngster tied a short piece of thread to that chunk of fish, in order to be able to trace it to its precise destination at the table. The newcomer, of course, having left the kitchen, knew nothing of this discreet sign.

At the *Shabbos* table, Zalmanyu observed the waiters closely, and sure enough, the marked piece of fish was being served to some stranger who was seated next to the newcomer. However, no sooner did he take it up than he was overcome by a feverish trembling and was unable to eat. He then pushed his plate aside—right in front of the newcomer, who duly ate it.

And that is how Zalmanyu removed all uncertainties as to the stature of his new colleague.

You Be the Teacher

Let's embark upon a story of the holy Zusya of Hanipol, when he visited *rebbe* Shmelke of Nikolsburg. Once, when Reb Zusya was visiting Reb Shmelke of Nikolsburg, he requested the latter to learn with him. Reb Shmelke responded, "If you teach me something from the secret wisdom I will teach you something from the revealed wisdom." Reb Zusya agreed and, in his characteristically holy and humble way, asked Reb Shmelke to teach him a *mishnah* word by word, and to translate it into *Yiddish* for him. Reb Shmelke began with *Brachos: me'eimatai korin et Hashema*, and translated for him, "From when do we say the *Shemah*?" Abruptly Reb Zusya threw himself to the ground in fear and trembling and questioned the holy rabbi, "How do you know that *me'eimatai* means 'from when'? Maybe it is from the word *eimah*, fear! 'From my fear' of *Hashem* I should say the *Shemah!*" At which Reb Shmelke said, "You be the teacher!"

Rabbi Moshe, son of Israel of Kozhnitz, explains, "This is how we can understand the fact that, when Korach mentioned *Hashem's* name, Moshe threw himself to the ground in fear of G-d, to demonstrate that one must mention *Hashem's* name in fear and trembling, and not out of discord or lightmindedness or hubris."

Prayer Without Movement

A *chassid* once queried of R' Pinchas as to why he prayed without making a sound and without moving his body, whereas the *davening* of other *rebbes*, was usually done in a loud voice accompanied by gestures of enthusiasm. R' Pinchas responded, "When a *tzaddik* prays, he cleaves in truth to *Hashem*, and loses all sense of corporeality, as if his very soul had departed from his body. The *gemarah* explains that in some people the soul leaves the body only after great agonies and convulsions, whereas in others it departs as quietly as one draws a hair out of milk or offers a kiss".

Who is Pursuing Whom?

Rabbi Pinchas of Koretz entered the *beis medrash*, and his disciples fell into a profound silence. He questioned, "What were you talking about just now?"

"We were saying how afraid we were that the *yetzer harah*, will pursue us."

"Don't worry," he blasted. "You haven't reached that point yet. Right now, you are still pursuing it!"

Don't Send Them Away

Reb Pinchus of Koretz, a very holy rabbi and follower of the Ba'al Shem Tov, became aggravated by the ever-increasing number of people who visited to ask for a blessing. News had gotten around that any person who needed help with problems for their health, children, or livelihood, that a blessing from Rabbi Pinchus seemed to aid. This brought a constant stream of people coming to Rabbi Pinchus, from far and near, to receive his holy blessing. Rabbi Pinchus was a rather quiet man who devoted to his time to the study of the holy *Torah*. Over time, interruptions from the people waiting for a blessing finally became so frustrating to him that he prayed for them to stop. "Dear *Hashem*, please make people hate me so they won't come anymore and disturb my studies." As we know, a prayer from such a holy man does not go unheeded. Sure enough, people began to feel repulsed by Rabbi Pinchus, and they stopped visiting him.

Alas, Rabbi Pinchus was content with his new-found freedom. Each day he immersed himself in his study of the holy *Torah*. It was not long until the holy day of *Succos* approached. The wife of Rabbi Pinchus, the *rebbetzin*, usually arranged to have someone's assistance to build their *succah*, but this year everyone was so repulsed by Rabbi Pinchus that they refused to come to her aid. As the day before *Succos* approached, a non-Jew reluctantly helped her and the *succah* was built just in time for the holiday.

The first evening of *Succos*, Rabbi Pinchus was seated in his *succah*, having a festive meal and studying the *Torah*. As he was enjoying his meal, an old man with a long white beard, and dressed in a long white robe, appeared at the door of the *succah*. Rabbi Pinchus recognized that it was the supernal guest, Avraham Avenu. Legend has it that a different supernal guest drops in the *succah* every night of *Succos*, known as the *ushpisin*. Avraham regularly comes on the first night.

"Avraham Avenu, please come into my *succah*," said Rabbi Pinchus excitedly. "Oh no," rebutted Avraham, "I only visit in *succahs* where there are guests." He then vanished.

Rabbi Pinchus got the hint. He realized that he was wrong for praying to be left alone. *Hashem* wants people to help each other more than study the holy *Torah*. So, he another time prayed to

Hashem, "Please forgive me." From that day forward, Rabbi Pinchus lent a ready ear and gave a strong blessing to anyone who approached him.

Don't Fool Yourselves

It is said that R' Pinchus used to warn his followers, "Never fool yourselves! Above all a Jew must be thoroughly honest with himself!" Once a student couldn't hold himself back and challenged him. "But *rebbe,*" he rebutted, "one who fools himself actually thinks he is being honest with himself. So how are we ever to know if we are being honest, or just fooling ourselves?"

"You have asked wisely, my son," the *rebbe* answered. "The answer, however, is simple. It is written in *Tanna d-Bei Eliyahu* that anyone who is careful to speak words of truth will be sent a *malach* who shows him the truth. One who speaks words of *sheker* will be sent a *malach* who fools and deceives him. So, if you will be careful to always tell the truth, you will never 'fool yourself.' If not, well ..."

This is a very telling incident as many of us live deceptive lives. Sometimes we deceive only ourselves, while other times we deceive others, yet we may not even have the faintest notion we are doing so. R' Pinchus also used to caution his disciples: "It is better to choke than to utter a lie."

Wait For it

Rav Pinchas of Koritz, was one of the first chassidic *rebbes*. Although he was penniless, asking another man for assistance was not his practice. Once, while he was walking to the *beis medrash,* he noticed a coin on the ground. He began to bend down to pick it up but paused. He thought for a moment and decided that it was negligent of him to bend down, for if *Hashem* wanted him to have the coin, He would have delivered it into his hand directly. So, he tossed the coin back to the ground, returning it to its path for which it was destined. Rav Pinchas continued on his way to the *beis medrash* and started learning. After some time, a wealthy man happened into the *beis medrash.* He looked around the room, scanning all the men engrossed in their *gemaras.* Finally, he approached Rav Koritz and told him, "While on the street I happened across this coin on the ground and I decided I would give it to someone in the *beis medrash*, the one who seems most virtuous in my eyes. Therefore, I offer it to you."

It Isn't Your Destiny to Go

Reb Refoel of Bershid, a learned *talmud chacham* and devoted follower of the Ba'al Shem Tov, yearned to settle in *Eretz Yisrael*. As was customary among *chassidim*, he sought the blessing of his *rebbe*, the Ba'al Shem Tov, before embarking. He told the *rebbe* about his plans and the *rav* responded with a clear no. He said, "*Eretz Yisrael* is *eretz hakodesh* only because the *Torah* makes it so. The holiness of *Eretz Yisrael* descends from Above to below; however, Poland needs you and the holy *Torah* you can teach here. So instead, you can create holiness from below to Above." It was made clear to Reb Refoel that he was not yet destined to settle in *Eretz Yisrael*. Even though he was disappointed, as a devoted *chassid* he accepted the Ba'al Shem Tov's advice without question. He thought, "Perhaps sometime in the future I will be able to fulfill my desire."

After many years had passed, Reb Refoel, who had served his community well as their rabbi, was now growing old. Once again, the desire to move to the holy land, stirred inside him. "I am too old to serve as a *rabbi*," he pondered, "and I would like very much to live out my remaining days in the holy land." For some reason, he refrained from requesting, for his blessing to work. Inside he just knew that the Ba'al Shem Tov would not approve. Thereafter he received a letter from his *rebbe*, again discouraging the move. There was no question in Reb Refoel's mind that the Ba'al Shem Tov knew of his renewed plan through his spiritual vision. Disappointed for the last time, Reb Refoel resolved to put the whole idea out of his mind once and for all. He dearly treasured the letter written by the holy land of the Ba'al Shem Tov, and he deposited it in a locked box that he put in a safe place.

Many years advanced after the Ba'al Shem Tov had already passed from this world. Reb Refoel, who was now very old and weak, returned to his previous yearnings for *aliyah* to the holy land. "This is my final chance to move to the holy land before my time is up to leave this world. He packed his belongings and put them on a wagon. Before departing, he invited his friends and relatives for a farewell meal. During the celebration, he walked outside the house to get a breath of fresh air. Even though it was not a windy day, suddenly from out of nowhere a piece of paper blew his way and fell at Reb Refoel's feet. He bent down to pick it up. Glancing at the paper in his hands, his face turned white with shock! It was none other than the Ba'al Shem Tov's letter that he had kept locked away for safekeeping all these years! How was it possible? He could not begin to guess, but he understood what had just occurred.

In dismay, Reb Refoel returned to his guests, and put the letter under the tablecloth. He then commenced to recount to his friends and relatives the entire history of his efforts to immigrate to the holy land. As he described how the Ba'al Shem Tov had sent him a letter, he reached beneath the tablecloth. To his amazement the letter had disappeared! Reb Refoel was dismayed. He simply couldn't believe it! He darted to the locked box where he had hidden the holy letter. The guests all hovered around with bated breath as he unlocked the box and raised the lid. Sure enough, the letter was still intact just as he had left it many years before.

"The relationship between a *chassid* and his *rebbe* transcends all worlds," he exclaimed passionately. "It is clear that my holy *rebbe*, the Ba'al Shem Tov, knew from the very first time I asked for his blessing, that it was not my destiny to reside in the Holy Land, but to remain here with all of you." Reb Refoel lived to a ripe old age, and continued to enlighten his community with his wisdom and teachings of *Torah*, as was his destiny.

Joy as a Segulah

The daughter of Rabbi Shmuel of Kaminka once visited the *tzaddik* Rabbi Raphael of Bershad, for a blessing to have children. Rabbi Raphael retorted, "Joy is a *segulah* for having children." When the daughter recounted his remarks to her father, he responded, "Rabbi Raphael learned this from the *Torah*, the Prophets, and the Writings. In the *Torah* it is written, 'And Sarah laughed' (Genesis 18:12), after which Isaac was born. In the Prophets, it is written, 'Sing out, O barren one' (Isaiah 54:1), while in the Writings, it is stated, 'A joyful mother of children.' (Psalms 113:9) That being the case, if Sarah laughed because it was a *segulah*, then why was *Hashem* angry with her?" Rabbi Shmuel rejoined, "We only need a *segulah* when a *tzaddik* promises us something. However, when the Holy One, blessed be He, is the One promising, we do not need a *segulah*. That is why He was angry with Sarah."

Just a Bite of Cheese

R' Yechiel Michel of Zlotchov once fell into a severe illness. One of his sons [Mordechai] departed without his father's knowledge, to request R' Pinchos Shapiro of Koritz to pray for his father's healing. R' Pinchos remarked to the son upon his arrival, "You are doubtless here about your father. Tell him that if he eats cheese he will recover." The son was surprised by the advice. "Who eats cheese as medicine?" he thought. R' Pinchos explained himself, "Your father stopped eating cheese as he wished to refrain from worldly pleasures. However, the angel appointed over cheese complained that until then, some of the cheese in this world was being utilized in R' Yechiel Michel's service of *Hashem*, and now it has stopped, for every morsel the *rav* consumes is a spiritual act— similar to the *Kohanim* eating *kadoshim* in the *Bais Hamikdosh*. His every bite is a *mitzvah*—like eating on *erev Yom Kippur*. Thus, his illness has come because he abstained from his great *mitzvah* of eating cheese. If he eats cheese, he will be cured." When the son returned from his adventure, R' Yechiel Michel already knew where he had been. Upon resuming to eat cheese, R' Yechiel Michel was indeed healed.

The Mezuzah Expense

The renowned Maharil, R' Yehoshua Leib Diskin who settled in Jerusalem, founded the Diskin Orphanage. He would have people go from house to house to examine the *mezuzos* of random people to see if they were properly *kosher*. When he came upon one that needed fixing, he paid the cost from the coffers of the orphanage. When R' Yehoshua Leib was questioned why he did this, he would reply, "You might think that this was an unnecessary, irrelevant expense for the institution. The opposite is true; it is income. The *Torah* guarantees, 'So that your days will increase.' If *kosher mezuzos* protect the people of Jerusalem and increase the days of its inhabitants, then there will be fewer orphans and the orphanage will have fewer expenses. Is this, then, not a form of income?"

The Leaky Boat

Always think ahead with kindness, as you never know what great *mitzvah* lies before you. Once, a man was hired to the beach port, in order to paint a boat. He brought with him his paint and brush. He began to paint the boat a bright, new red, as requested of him. As he painted the boat, he observed that the paint was seeping through the bottom of the boat. Realizing that there was a leak, he decided on his own to mend it. When the painting was done, he collected his money for the job and went his way. The subsequent day, the owner of the boat came to the painter and presented him with a huge check. The painter was taken back. "You have already reimbursed me for painting the boat," he remarked. "But this is not for the paint job. It is for mending the leak in the boat." Responded the painter, "Oh, that was so minor a thing that I had no plans to even charge for it. Surely you are not thinking to pay me this large amount for such a petty thing?" With a heartfelt voice, the boat owner said, "My dear friend, you do not understand. Let me tell you what happened. When I asked you to paint the boat, I had forgotten to mention to you about the leak. After the boat was nice and dry, my children took the boat and went fishing. When I heard that they had gone out in the boat I was frantic, for I remembered that the boat had a leak! Now just imagine my relief and happiness when I saw them returning safe and sound! I inspected the boat and saw that you had repaired the leak! Now, can't you appreciate what you have done? You have saved the lives of my children! There isn't enough money to repay you for your good 'little' deed." With that he pushed the check into the painter's hand with a hearty smile.

It is Not Slippery to Me

It was during the winter of 5663 (1903), when I accompanied my father for the couple of months he spent consulting medical specialists in Vienna. He would sometimes go out in the evening to visit the *shtieblach* of the local Polish Jews, to be among *chassidim*. He wanted to hear stories directly from their mouths, to listen to a chassidic saying, and to observe their fine conduct and refined character. It was Wednesday night, on the eve of the fifteenth of the month of *Shevat*, that my father visited one of these *shtiblach*. There were several hoary *chassidim* sitting around together, talking. As my father and I drew closer, we heard that they were telling stories of the saintly Rabbi Meir of Premishlan. One of the tales they related was about the *mikvah* of Rabbi Meir's neighborhood that stood at the foot of a steep mountain. Whenever the slippery weather came, everyone had to walk all the way around for fear of slipping on the mountain path and breaking their bones. However, that was everyone apart from Rabbi Meir, who simply walked down that path whatever the weather, and never did he lose his footing. On one icy day, Rabbi Meir embarked as usual to take the direct route to the *mikvah*. Two guests were staying in the area, sons of the rich who had come somewhat under the influence of the "Enlightenment" movement. These two young men were unable to believe in the supernatural achievements of the *rabbis*. So, when they noticed Rabbi Meir striding downhill with confidence, they decided to demonstrate that they too could negotiate the hazardous path with ease. The moment Rabbi Meir entered the *mikvah* building, they took to the road. It didn't take more than a few steps before they stumbled and slipped, needing medical treatment for their many injuries. After recovering, one of them, the son of one of Rabbi Meir's close *chassidim*, mustered the courage to approach the *tzaddik* with the obvious question, "Why was it that no man could cope with that treacherous path, yet the *rabbi* never stumbled?" Answered Rabbi Meir, "If a man is bound up on high, he doesn't fall down below. Meir'l is bound up on high, and that is why he can go up and down, even on a slippery hill."

Ruach Hakodesh is Drawn Only From the *Torah*

The Seer of Lublin attributed his *ruach hakodesh* to his *Torah* study. While still a child, the Divrei Chaim of Sanz became a student of the Seer. One day, as the Seer was receiving a lengthy line of *chassidim*, giving them advice and helping them with their problems, he suddenly stopped and asked everyone accept the Divrei Chaim to leave the room. He locked the door and then spent several minutes reciting *mishnayos* by heart. Then he turned to the Divrei Chaim and explained.

"Years ago, when a Jew needed advice, he would go to the *Kohen Hagadol*, who would inquire of the *urim v'tumim*. But today a Jew goes to a *Torah* scholar for guidance. To those scholars who learn *Torah* for its own sake, the hidden light of the *Torah* is revealed. Then they can see answers to all problems. But, sometimes, dealing with their congregation weakens their connection to the *Torah* and they lose this inner light. Thus, I closed the door and studied some *mishnayos*, to renew my attachment to the *Torah*. Why am I telling you this? Because, one day, you too will be a leader of Israel. Therefore, you must know that *ruach hakodesh* is drawn only from the *Torah*."

The Seer found a hint to this in the verse, "And [Avraham] sat in the door of his tent in the heat of the day." (*Bereshis* 18:1) When one learns *Torah* with burning desire, one opens the door to Divine illumination.

A Vision Only to See Good

The *chassidim* tell over that the Seer's gaze originally encompassed the entire world. However, unable to bear this power, and in order not to see the bad in the people of Israel, he prayed to *Hashem* to recant his holy power. Hearing his pleas however, *Hashem* answered only half of his request. He drastically reduced the Seer's ability, and he allowed him still to see clearly for a distance of 1,600 miles. Beyond that, his vision now turned dim. Still unable to bear this power, he begged Reb Mordechai of Neschiz to pray that *Hashem* should remove the rest, but Reb Mordechai turned him down. *Hashem* had given the Seer this for a reason, and he was obligated to use it for good. Still he treated every Jew he met, righteous or not, as if he were a *tzaddik*, as if he truly saw only the good in them.

"How beautiful are the Jews," he would often remark.

Upon learning a person's problems, the Seer would never be judgmental. He would rather seek to lessen the punishment of the Heavenly Court. He said, "When a Jew is crushed by suffering you must never say that he deserves it. Instead, you must pray for him and save him. Do not justify Divine decrees, instead, beg *Hashem* to annul them and send only goodness and kindness to Israel."

Getting His Hands Dirty

A beggar knocked on the Seer's door. The Seer personally invited him in, fed him, and even cleaned up the table after him. That was too much for the Seer's students. "We can understand that our *rebbe* wants the *mitzvah* of feeding the poor, but does he also have to clean the table? He has attendants to do that." The Seer overheard them and commented, "When the *Kohen Hagadol* finished with his holy service on *Yom Kippur*, he still went back into the Holy of Holies to retrieve the incense spoon he had left there. That too was an *avodah*, and he didn't send his attendant to do it for him!"

Tossed From the Window

Napoleon Bonaparte had begun his surge across Eastern Europe, towards Russia. Three of the top *tzaddikim* of that generation – the Seer of Lubin, the Maggid of Kozhnitz and Reb Menachem Mendel of Rimanov – joined together to attempt to use the incursion to hasten the redemption. Attempting to use their great spiritual powers, they sought to convert the Napoleonic wars into the battle of *Gog* and *Magog* that heralds the coming of the *Moshiach*. It was a pathway fraught with danger, and success was far from assured. "If we have a joyful *Simchas Torah*," the Seer confided in his *chassidim*, "we will have a joyful *Tishah b' Av*."

That *Simchas Torah* night, he ordered his followers to dance with all their strength. He summoned a small group aside and cautioned them, "Do not take your eyes off me for a moment; the forces of evil are out to stop our holy work." Then he went into his room on the second floor of the *shul* for a moment. Suddenly, the door slammed shut by itself. When the *chassidim* pried it open, they discovered the room empty! Only a small window was open.

The *chassidim* scurried out into the snow to search for their *rebbe* but could not locate him. After several hours, Reb Eliezer of Chelmnik overheard someone groaning. "Who is there?" he called. "Reb Yaakov Yitzchok ben Matil," came the response. Reb Eliezer gave a scream and the other *chassidim* came running to see what happened. Indeed, the Seer had been thrown a great distance from the shul but, somehow, he was okay. The *chassidim* managed to carry him back to the shul. Reb Shmuel of Karov held the Seer's head. The

Seer was murmuring something... *Tikkun Chatzos*, dirges bemoaning the destruction of the Holy Temple!

Afterwards, the Seer moaned, "Why didn't you divulge to me that the Kozhnitzer Maggid had passed away? If I knew that, I would certainly not have attempted what I did. All the influences of evil rose up against me. If not for the Kozhnitzer Maggid descending from the Upper Worlds to save me by spreading his *tallis* under me to cushion my fall, I would have been dead by now."

Hence, the *chassidim* did not have a joyful *Simchas Torah*, and their *Tishah b'Av* was distressing. The redemption did not come, and the Seer passed away that very *Tishah b'Av*.

Rebbetzin Matil Feigeh had grown up in the town of Lublin. She once stated to her grandson, Reb Pinchas Dovid, the first Bostoner Rebbe, that as a youngster she had once visited the study of the Seer of Lublin. Curious, she went to the room of the Seer and saw the window through which he had been hurled. Although she was just a little girl at the time, the window was so slender that even she was unable to pass through it!

I Have Everything

One of Reb Nota of Chelm's rich *chassidim* once came to him with a strange complaint: "Rebbe, I have everything I want in life: children, health and livelihood."

"So, what is wrong?" Reb Nota asked.

"This is precisely the problem," the chassid continued. "I know I am not a *tzaddik*. So why should I deserve all this? I must be receiving my future reward now. Perhaps, *chas v' shalom*, *Hashem* does not want to reward me in the World to Come!"

"But don't you wear eyeglasses?" Reb Nota reassured him. "Don't they cause you suffering? Sometimes you forget them. Sometimes they break. You are not living your World to Come; your glasses cause you suffering enough!"

A Young Rebbe's Blessing

One early morning, when Reb Dovid of Lelov was still a youngster of five or six, he went to the local bakery and asked for a small favor. He required a roll on credit because his family was very underprivileged. The baker, being a friendly fellow, gladly gave the young child the roll. No sooner had Dovid departed the shop than the dough in the baker's oven begin to rise over the edges of the baking pans and poured down the sides. The baker was unable to bring enough pans to seize all of it, so powerful was the blessing that had permeated the dough.

He Thinks He Knows Me

When Rav Shlomo of Zalshin was leaving on a trip to Lelov, a neighbor requested of him to take a block of cheese to Reb Dovid. "I know the *rebbe*," he petitioned. "Please, tell him this gift is from me." When Rav Shlomo transmitted the man's words, Reb Dovid said, "He only thinks he knows me. By the time I was nine years old, even the angels in Heaven knew nothing of me!"

Hidden From Even His Rebbe

So hidden were the ways of Reb Dovid, that even the penetrating eyes of his *rebbe*, the Seer of Lublin, could not fathom his capabilities. A short while before Reb Dovid of Lelov passed away, his *chassidim* observed that he was laughing. "I've hidden myself so well," he went on to explain, "that even the Seer doesn't realize what I am." Normally a *chassid* wants to appear great in the eyes of his *rabbi*, so he can get respect from those around him, but not Reb Dovid. Later, after his passing, the Seer beheld him in a dream, burning like fire and shining with a great light. "I never knew he was so great," the Seer later told his followers.

Giving Away His Coat

Being humble was not Reb Dovid of Lelov's only virtue; his kindness and humility were apparent even from his youth. His family was so poverty-stricken that his father had to struggle considerably just to purchase for him a winter coat. Reb Dovid was very excited to receive it, so he could be warm like the other children. However, the very next day, on his way to school, he noticed a small boy in torn clothes standing in the chill and crying from the cold. Reb

Dovid didn't think twice, and immediately removed his new coat, and offered it to the boy. Having returned from *cheder*, his mother enquired sympathetically, "Dovid, what happened? Where is your new coat?"

"I gave it to a poor boy who needed it," he retorted.

"What? Quick, eat your lunch and run back to school before your father comes home. If he catches you without that coat, he will give you quite a spanking."

"That's all right mother," young Dovid said in all seriousness. "If spanking me would make father feel better, then let him."

Strange Teshuva

Reb Dovid, as a young man residing in his father-in-law's house, practiced a severe regimen of self-affliction. His father-in-law, a simple gentleman, could not appreciate such strange behavior. When he learned how Reb Dovid would immerse himself in frozen lakes, or roll naked in the snow as atonement, he became enraged. As it continued to get under his nerves, he threw Reb Dovid out of the house. One of the servants observing what happened, let him back in through a rear door. Yet, he too, was bewildered by Reb Dovid's strange actions. "Have you really sinned so much that you must afflict yourself so?" he questioned.

"What can I do?" responded Reb Dovid. "I still have not reached the level of complete love for all Jews."

Who's Driving the Wagon

During the old days, it wasn't uncommon for yeshiva students, even after they were married, to spend the weekdays at yeshiva rather than at home. In the early years of Reb Dovid of Lelov's marriage, he studied in an out-of-town *beis medrash*, returning to his father-in-law's house only for *Shabbos*. During his return home, he accepted a lift from a Jewish wagon driver. While in the middle of the journey, their horse abruptly stood still. The wagon driver stroked the horse with his whip, but it declined to budge. Reb Dovid directed the driver, "Tie the reins to the wagon, and come down into the carriage with me. Let the horse go where it wants, *Hashem* will help us reach our destination." The wagon driver had nothing to lose and did as he was told. Amazingly, the horse took off like lightning, only to stop a few minutes later. They were already outside Reb Dovid's home!

The wagon driver could not hold himself back; he went inside excitedly and related to the whole family about their miraculous journey. Only then did Reb Dovid's father-in-law finally begin to recognize who his son-in-law really was and appreciate him.

Who is the Lowliest Jew in Town

When Reb Elimelech first encountered Reb Dovid of Lelov, he immediately recognized his potential. So, he began without delay, by teaching him a lesson in true humility. When Reb Dovid arrived at the *beis medresh*, he found himself behind the extensive line of *chassidim* waiting for their chance to greet the *tzaddik*. He procured his place in line, and ultimately his turn arrived.

"Where are you from?" the *rebbe* questioned.

"From Bialeh, a small town."

"And what do you do?"

"I am the *rav* of the town."

"And who is the lowliest Jew in the town?"

Reb Dovid was dumbfounded by the unexpected question but, before he could respond, the *rebbe* had now turned to the next person in line. Reb Dovid was confused. Was all his elaborate preparation for naught? It must be a mistake, he thought to himself. He would just try again tomorrow and meeting the *rebbe* would be all that he hoped for.

The following day, he yet again waited in line and, when his turn came, the *rebbe* asked him the identical question: "Who is the lowliest Jew in your town?"

Reb Dovid was ready for it this time and began to explain, "As *rav* of the city, most of my time is spent with the learned Jews in the synagogue. I am not familiar with every Jew in town, especially the lower elements." However, the *rebbe* had already turned to the next person in line.

"Perhaps the *rebbe* is simply testing my *ahavas Yisrael*, my love of all Jews," Reb Dovid resolved. The following day, Friday, Reb

Dovid once more took his place in line. Once more was asked the same question: "Who is the lowliest Jew in your town?"

"*Rebbe*, I cannot know what is in the heart of every Jew, nor am I fit to pass judgement. I don't..." But the *rebbe* already skipped to the next *Yiddala*, giving a hearty *shalom*.

Having lost all hope this time, Reb Dovid dejectedly returned to his chambers. What could he do, where could he go? All his trip was for naught. *Shabbos* was approaching now and there wasn't enough time to return home. So, he decided to pray alone in his room, for if he prayed in the *beis medrash*, he knew what to expect. Every person would file past the *rebbe* to receive a *gut Shabbos*, while he would be asked the same embarrassing question, for which he hadn't a new response.

Brokenhearted, he started to *daven Mincha*. Towards the conclusion of his prayers, he suddenly thought: "Who is the lowliest Jew in my town? It's me! I'm the lowliest Jew in my town. All the other Jews are happily welcoming the *Shabbos* in *shul*, while I pray alone here in this tiny hotel room, far away from home. Surely, I must be the worst of all!

Suddenly, there was a loud knock at the door. Surprisingly, the *rebbe's gabbai* had arrived to invite him to pray in the *beis medrash* with the *rebbe*. When he arrived the *rebbe* turned to him with a glowing smile, "Now that you know – *Shalom Aleichem*!" From that point on, Reb Dovid became one of the Reb Elimelech's closest disciples.

Feeling the Shabbos in One's Veins

While in Lizhenzsk, Reb Dovid of Lelov heard that the Seer of Lublin had arrived. He was so excited, and he sprinted to his tavern to greet him. Since *Shabbos* was rapidly approaching, Reb Dovid quickly turned to leave. The Seer stopped him to question him. "You seem very worried about the *Shabbos*. Do you really know precisely when it arrives?"

"Of course," responded Reb Dovid. "When *Shabbos* draws near, the veins in my hand start to throb with fear." He drew up his sleeve and disclosed them to the Seer. "Then what do you think of this story?" the Seer revealed, telling Reb Dovid a superficially meaningless parable with reference to a farmer and a king's daughter. Understanding it in a deeper sense, Reb Dovid took a shot at explaining it. "It seems to be an allegory for the following Kabbalistic teaching of the *Arizal*." The Seer was so delighted with Reb Dovid's response that he hugged him and said, "From now on, you are one of my men." Thus, even while remaining a disciple of the Reb Elimelech, Reb Dovid often visited the Seer in Lizhenzsk.

Helping One's Competitor

Reb Dovid of Lelov maintained himself with a small grocery store. On one occasion, a customer arrived at the shop and inquired where he could buy salt. Reb Dovid first listed all the other storehouses in town, and only afterwards concluded, "And you can buy it here, if you like." A different morning, when he arrived at his store, he observed that his competitor's store had not yet opened yet. He hurried to wake him. "Get up quickly!" he urged. "Customers are already coming!"

One day, Reb Dovid of Lelov decided to close his little shop for good. He explained his reasoning rather simply. "When I see a customer go to my competitor's store, I'm delighted that he is making a living. But I recently realized that not everyone feels this way. Whenever a customer comes into my store, I may actually be causing my competitor anguish! So, I had to close my shop. How could I cause another Jew pain?"

Reb Dovid's son, Reb Moshe, also had his own shop for work. On one occasion, he complained about a competitor across the street, who was stealing his customers with a similar store. "True, you may lose money," Reb Dovid rejoined. "But isn't it wonderful to see your neighbor making such a good living?"

Pray for Everyone

Reb Dovid of Lelov once remarked, "Why do people think of me as a *tzaddik*? I still love my own family more than the rest of the Jewish people."

At one time, Reb Dovid's young son became sick, the *chassidim* gathered to pray on his behalf. Reb Dovid overheard them and began to cry. "Why are you crying?" they asked, wondering why he was so emotional. "Your son will get better."

"I'm crying," he retorted, "because we don't pray so intensely when someone else's son gets sick!"

The Promise

During the early hours of the morning, a passing Jew noticed a man lying unconscious on the frozen riverbank. It was Reb Dovid of Lelov, who had fainted from the severe cold as he left the frigid *mikvah* water. Hoping to revive him, the man wrapped Reb Dovid in his own coat and carried him to his own home. He laid him in his bed and cared for him until he revived.

"You saved my life," Reb Dovid told him. "What should I bless you with? Wealth or the World to Come?"

"The World to Come."

"If so, I will appear to you before you die," Reb Dovid promised him before leaving.

Many years passed by, and Reb Dovid left this world for the next. His rescuer also grew old, and eventually his condition deteriorated. One *Shabbos* day, he seemed to be on the verge of death. The *chevrah kaddishah*, turned up to attend to him in his last moments but, when they arrived, he confidently told them, "Go away, my time has not yet come." Right after *Shabbos* however, he sent for them to return. "Now my time has come," he told them. With his last breaths at hand, he shared with them the story of the *rebbe's* promise.

"When you came to me earlier, I turned my face to the wall and prayed to see Reb Dovid. The holy ministering angels went to call him, but he refused to come during *Shabbos*. But just now he came, so I must say my final confession."

It Must be Returned

A poor man on one occasion came to visit Reb Dovid of Lelov for advice. He was crying about his misfortune. Apparently, his house had been broken into and his meager possessions – his wallet, his *tallis* and *tefillin*, and a few other items – had been stolen. He had almost nothing left. Reb Dovid calmed the man down with his sweet voice and requested of him to wait a little bit. Taking the spiritual responsibility to help his fellow, he then went out in the bitter winter cold and broke a hole in the ice. He immersed himself again and again in the frozen water *mikvah*, until his attendant became concerned. "*Rebbe*, please come out of there. You'll get sick!" Nevertheless, Reb Dovid refused to listen to his calls. "I'm not coming out until my prayers are accepted and that poor man's belongings are restored," he retorted.

Some minutes later, Reb Dovid left the water, and returned home with his attendant. The unfortunate man was still sitting there not knowing what to do. After a few minutes, there was a loud knock at the door. "Open up! Open up!" shouted a rough voice in desperation. They opened the door slightly and someone – they could not see who it was – threw in a package containing all the poor man's belongings and thereafter scurried away into the night.

There are No Bad Jews

Reb Dovid of Lelov often said, "Every Jew has a core of complete goodness, even if he himself is unaware of it. The bad is only external, not intrinsic to his soul at all." The inner Jewish soul is simply not inclined to sin.

"It is impossible to find bad in a Jew," Reb Dovid explained.

Two Yuddin

Reb Dovid on one occasion overheard a simple Jew praying. Between each verse the *Yiddala* would say *Hashem*'s Name. Reb Dovid enquired of the man why. The man explained, "I've heard that two *yuds* printed together are an abbreviation for *Hashem's* Name ("). See," he showed him. "They are printed between every sentence in my prayer book."

Reb Dovid gently explained to the man, "No, sometimes two dots are just the end of a sentence, and sometimes they are *Hashem's* Name." As he related the story, Reb Dovid further explained to his students, "Whenever you have two *yuddin* or two *Yiddin* standing one beside the other, treating each other equally, the *Shechinah* rests between them, and they form *Hashem's* Name. But whenever one *Yid* thinks he is higher than the next, they don't form *Hashem's* Name!"

A Modest Man's Home

Reb Dovid's "house" was a single small room. As most *rebbes* do, besides hosting his family, they also entertained guests. He explained to his *chassidim* once. "If a piece of string is considered a wall for the making of an *eruv* for *Shabbos*," he continued serenely, "it can create a private room for me as well." Therefore, whenever he needed privacy, he simply cordoned off one corner of the room with a piece of string.

In Vain Do You Rise Early

Wherever he would go, Reb Dovid of Lelov had an impact on people. Once he arrived in a certain town in the wee hours of the morning. Only one shop was open, and all the other competitors were closed. "Certainly," Reb Dovid thought, "the owner has risen early to study a little before daybreak." However, when Reb Dovid entered, it was surprising for him to find the owner standing idly behind the counter.

"Why open your shop so early?" Reb Dovid enquired. The man clarified that his livelihood was suffering from his competitors. Therefore, he decided to open his store before them to attract early customers. Reb Dovid was appalled by the man's absence of faith. He raised his hands in disbelief and parroted the Psalmist, "In vain do you rise early, sit up late, and eat the bread of toil, for to His beloved [*Hashem*] gives tranquility." (Psalms 127:2) Then Reb Dovid walked out the door moving on to his next adventure. The man later testified that throughout that entire day, not even one customer entered his store. Reb Dovid's message was not just for the shopkeeper but for all of us, to realize that faith in *Hashem* is fundamental to success. It isn't always about how hard we work but if we truly believe who it is that is really providing.

A Spring of Water

A similar story teaches us another lesson about faith. Reb Dovid of Lelov was once traveling near the town of Bialeh. He was extremely thirsty, but there was no water to be found. "Master of the Universe," he called out, "Moshe Rabbeinu hit a rock and water flowed out. I fully believe it can happen again." He stuck the end of his walking stick into the ground, and when he removed it, water flowed from the hole. He took a vessel and drank to satisfaction.

Truly Modest Learning

There are many great sages, but a true *chassid* keeps much of his piety to himself. Reb Dovid of Lelov tried to hide his true greatness in *Torah*, even from those near to him. In fact, for much of his life, no one ever saw him studying. He would hide in the attic to be undisturbed. During the depths of the winter, he would wrap his feet with pillows and continue learning through the cold. Whenever he heard someone coming up the stairs and approaching, he would hurriedly put away his book.

One time, Reb Dovid's brother-in-law, Rabbi Chaim Beldechovitz, came for a visit. Having no room downstairs, Reb Dovid prepared a bed for him in the attic. Reb Chaim, anxious to observe his brother-in-law studying, only pretended to fall asleep. Later that night, Reb Dovid climbed up to the attic and opened a *Tikunei Zohar*. Suspecting something, he arose and approached the bed. With a whisper or maybe a prayer, he said, "Chaim, aren't you asleep yet?" A heavy slumber suddenly fell upon the young man, who saw nothing of Reb Dovid's nighttime activities.

Hidden Brilliance

According to the Chidushei Harim, when Reb Dovid of Lelov was only twenty-five years old; he had already learned the entire *Talmud* twenty-four times. Yet his close friend and *mechutan*, the Yehudi Hakodesh, knew nothing about his brilliance. One day when he found out of Reb Dovid's brilliance in *Torah*, he jumped onto the table and started dancing for joy.

The Talmud is Still Alive

Reb Dovid of Lelov once happened upon his son, Reb Moshe, in the *beis medrash* pondering a *blatt* of *gemarah*, on a purely intellectual level. To make his point, he went over to him and closed the *gemarah*. "This is not how one learns," his father said.

How then does one learn?

Another tale might shed some more light. It was the habit of Reb Dovid to test his grandson, Reb Yosef Hirsh, every *Shabbos*. One time, Reb Dovid being dissatisfied with his grandson's learning. His grandson Reb Yosef reviewed the material a second time, but Reb Dovid was still not pleased.

Reb Yosef Hirsh began to shed tears. "If I don't know it by now, I will never know it!"

"You understand the material fine," explained Reb Dovid, "But you lack something else. When you learn the *gemarah*, and mention the name of the sage, it's not enough to know what he said. You must see him standing in front of you as if he were still alive."

Reb Dovid's Kiddush Cup

Among his last wishes, Reb Dovid of Lelov asked that his *kiddush* cup be sent to the Seer in Lublin, as a remembrance after he passed. That Friday night, the Seer of Lublin selected Reb Dovid's cup to make *kiddush* (to increase his merit), but suddenly, his hand began to shake. He was forced to put the cup down. He tried again to hold it but to no avail. He had no choice but to put it down once more. "What a loss, what a loss," he groaned. "He will never be forgotten." It wasn't until now that even the great *rebbe*, known as the Seer, who could see all things, realized his student's greatness. So well did Reb Dovid hide his spiritual achievements.

The Light Lives On

It is a tradition to keep a memorial light burning, at all times, next to the grave of a holy *rabbi*. So, it was at the cemetery vault of Reb Dovid of Lelov. The caretaker would relight the oil wick daily. On one occasion, the caretaker returned from a lengthy trip and realized that he had forgotten to arrange for someone to replenish the oil in his stead. When he entered the vault, ready to rekindle the flame, he found the light still burning brightly – even though there was no oil remaining in the glass cup! Obviously, the light of Reb Dovid's *Torah* will never be extinguished. Like the golden menorah in the holy Temple that was never extinguished, Reb Dovid's light lives on.

Tefillin on Fire

Reb Dovid of Lelov's *tefillin* were not ordinary *tefillin*, but especially written for Reb Dovid by the Ohr Pnei Moshe, Reb Moshe of Pshivorsk. It is spoken that when that *tzaddik* wrote *tefillin*, fire would flash from the letters.

Reb Dovid had once traveled to Pshivorsk on the recommendation of the Seer of Lublin. When he arrived, the Ohr Pnei Moshe was engrossed in writing a pair of *tefillin*. Therefore, he did not return Reb Dovid's greeting, for according to the *Kabbalah*, one must not speak in the middle of writing. When finished, he turned to Reb Dovid.

"*Shalom Aleichem*. Where are you from?"

"From Lelov," Reb Dovid replied.

"And your name?"

"Dovid."

"I see. Then you must be the Reb Dovid of Lelov that Eliyahu Hanavi told me about. He told me to write two pairs of *tefillin* for you." Reb Moshe went over to his cabinet, took out two pairs of *tefillin* (Rashi and Rabbeinu Tam) and handed them to Reb Dovid. They were already wrapped in paper with his name written on it!

The Tefillin Continues on

Eventually, these special *tefillin* were passed on and ended up in the hands of Reb Dovid Yitzchok of Zarick. Once a fire broke out in Zarick and quickly consumed the flammable, wooden houses of the town. Everyone ran for their lives. Even though he grabbed his *tefillin* and ran to the small cemetery on the outskirts of the city, when the fire reached there, he forgot them as he ran in haste for cover. When he returned after the fire, he found the bag and its *tallis* completely burned, while the *tefillin* were unsinged in their cases!

The Ohr Pnei Moshe had promised that any *tefillin* he wrote would stay *kosher* forever. I guess they also have an added protection of being fire proof.

Look Under Your Own Feet

Reb Simcha Bunim of Pshischah and Rebbe Nachman of Breslov both had the habit of telling over this story to their followers when they met them for the first time:

There was once a poor man by the name of Reb Isaac ben Yakil, of Krakow. He lived impoverished for several years, not knowing where his next crust of bread would come from. Even so, Reb Isaac had absolute faith that *Hashem* would not allow him to starve, and that one day his misery would conclude.

As he fell to sleep one night, he dreamed that there was a highly valuable, buried treasure under a specific bridge in Prague. At first, he didn't take the dream very seriously, assuming it was just his wishful thinking. After all, who doesn't dream of finding a treasure and becoming rich? However, when the dream kept repeating itself, night after night after night, he couldn't help but reconsider. Perhaps there was something to it? Could it possibly be true?

So, one day he set off to Prague, a long and tiring journey, curious to see how things would fall into play. When he arrived, he discovered that the bridge was right near the royal palace and thus heavily guarded at all hours. Up and down soldiers would march, alert and ready for any unusual activity. Digging under the bridge was clearly out of the question. Oh, how disappointing. He had traveled so far.

A fighter by nature, Reb Isaac was not going to give up that easily on his dream. Daily he returned to the bridge to think of some way he could search for the treasure. One day, one of the guards recognized him. Soon he became curious as well. "Why do you come to the bridge every day?" he asked him. "Are you waiting for someone?"

Reb Isaac had nothing to lose at this point, as it was clear he couldn't dig up the treasure alone. He also knew that the guard wouldn't believe some half-hearted excuse, so he confessed his dream. The guard listened, threw back his head, and laughed heartily. "You came all this way because of a silly dream? You are so foolish," he retorted. "I had a similar dream that a certain Jew has a buried treasure under his stove, but do you see me going on a wild goose chase over a silly dream? Of course not!" and he laughed.

Realizing the message from *Hashem*, Reb Isaac scurried off to buy a ticket for the first train back to Krakow. Now he knew where to look for the treasure. Sure enough, when he returned he straightaway shoved the iron stove out of the way and began digging at the solid dirt floor. It wasn't long after, to his boundless joy and astonishment, that some gold coins emerged!

As a truly devout Jew, he used the money from the treasure to build a magnificent synagogue which bore his name. With the rest of the money he built himself a comfortable home and furnished it well.

When Reb Bunim told this saga to followers who had travelled from far and wide to visit him, what was truly the message he was trying to relate? You don't always find what you're looking for by travelling to a distant chassidic court. True spiritual treasure can be acquired right near home, with intense effort and devout prayer.

Furthermore, many of us try to change our location or situation, in order to find happiness. True happiness is realizing you already have everything you need.

Hiding Their Poverty

Reb Elazar Mendel and his wife never complained and kept hidden their difficulties from others. Every Friday afternoon, when other families prepared hot food for *Shabbos,* Rebbetzin Matil Feigeh put a pot of boing water on the stove to make it appear that they were also cooking.

One day, a neighbor entered her house and looked in her pot, and all she saw was boiling water!

The neighbor ran straight to the head of the charity in Jerusalem and put the family on the community's distribution list.

It Could Be Sha'atnez

Reb Daniel was dwelling in the holy city of Jerusalem. His entire life was devoted to *Torah* study, despite the severe poverty that had plagued him ever since leaving his native Lomzha. He and his wife were raising their seven children in a dilapidated two-room apartment. Even through their troubles, at almost any time of day or night, you could find Reb Daniel poring over a book of *Talmud.* Rarely did he leave his room.

His piety wasn't news to his neighbors; they recognized him as a great scholar. Reb Daniel's wife had once mentioned the promise her father had extracted from her before he died. That she always be a true "helpmate" to her husband, and never disturb his learning.

Her husband was virtually never seen on the street, as she did everything she could to help him study, thus fulfilling her father's wishes. Her husband never went to the marketplace or ran an errand. Rarely did he even step outside for a breath of fresh air.

Due to his devotions, sightings of Reb Daniel were quite unusual. So, one day, when he was spotted hurrying through the marketplace with a bulky sack on his shoulder, everyone took notice. What was Reb Daniel doing out here?

It turned out that a day earlier, a peddler had appeared at the door selling secondhand clothing. Reb Daniel's wife was about to purchase some garments when her husband reminded her of *mitzvah* of *sha'atnez* (the prohibition against wearing clothes woven of wool and flax). Instantly she ran to fetch her neighbor's husband, Reb Shmuel Zanvil, who was proficient in such matters. However, when he examined the clothes, it was discovered that several indeed contained *sha'atnez*. She was forced to decline the purchase and the peddler left.

The following day, Reb Daniel asked her about the clothes, wondering if the problem was resolved, since at the time he was immersed in his studies. "Oh, there was *sha'atnez* in them, so I gave them back," she explained. "What?" Reb Daniel called out in surprise. "G-d forbid, another Jew might inadvertently buy them!"

He tossed on his shoes and raced from house to house in search of the peddler, eventually locating him in the marketplace trying to sell his wares. Feeling relieved, he learned that the peddler hadn't succeeded in selling even one garment. Wanting to be sure that would remain the case, he purchased the entire lot just to get rid of it, even though they were a family that struggled to pay day to day bills. But that was the type of pious person Reb Daniel was.

Never Too Tired to Pray With all Your Strength

Reb Elazar Mendel prayed with such intensity, that the entire congregation could feel it and trembled. At times, even the inanimate objects in the room would shake. When he finished praying, you could find him drenched in sweat. Just on the blessings of *Krias Shemah*, it could take him several hours. On *Rosh Hashanah*, it took Reb Elazar Mendel five hours alone, just to recite the *Shemoneh Esrei.*

One of his supporters confessed the following story: "A group of us once traveled with the *rebbe* to Chevron. We journeyed by mule team, over mountains and valleys, hard rocks and arid plains. It was an arduous journey which took the entire day. We arrived in Chevron after nightfall, exhausted to the point of collapse. Every bone in our bodies was sore. After such torture, we assumed that the *rebbe* would not extend his evening prayers, but he spent three hours praying *Shemoneh Esrei*. When he stepped back, as he finished, he muttered to himself, 'Was that a prayer? Better to pray again as a free-will offering' (*Orech Chaim* 106:1). Without a moment's pause, he re-entered *Shemoneh Esrei* and stood there until dawn."

Is it Kosher

At some point, Reb Elazar Mendel called in the local Jewish milkman. "Are you sure this milk is from your herd?" he questioned. "Of course," the man replied in defense. "Would I give the *rebbe* non-Jewish milk?" Reb Elazar Mendel said nothing in return but declined to drink the milk. The following day, Reb Elazar Mendel queried the milkman again, receiving the same reply.

On the third day, Reb Elazar Mendel had enough. He summoned the milkman into his private study. "If you do not confess the truth," he cautioned, "you will suffer dearly." The milkman became so frightened that he admitted his wrongdoings. He had been selling non-Jewish milk for the past few days. "No one in the world knew this but the *rebbe*," he stated. An angel from Heaven must have told him!"

One *Shabbos* evening, Reb Elazar Mendel picked up his *kiddush* cup, and then returned it to the table. Once again, he picked it up and placed it right back down. This happened a few more times. "Tell me, Dovid'l," he asked his young son. "You bought the wine. Are you sure nothing happened to it?"

The son answered, "Nothing, father. I bought it at the usual store, and I held it tightly until I got home. Even though an Arab boy followed me, I never let the bottle out of my hand."

Reb Elazar Mendel asked a few more detailed questions to see if anything was amiss. Finally, he discovered that the Arab boy had moved the bottle, rending its contents unfit.

The Levi or Maybe Not

Since it was a small *shul*, there was just one *Levi* in Reb Elazar Mendel's to call up to the *Torah*. Whenever the *Torah* was recited in public, he received the second *aliyah*. Every time he got his *aliyah* to the *Torah*, Reb Elazar Mendel would smile slightly, but no one understood the reason behind it. Several years later the *Levi* became deathly ill and lay on his sickbed. Reb Elazar Mendel visited him at his bedside and said to him, "Now you can tell the truth. Are you really a *Levi*?"

"No," the man admitted after so many years. "In Europe, I had heard that the Jews here look badly upon new immigrants and refuse to call them up to the *Torah*. By calling myself a *Levi*, I guaranteed that I would always get an *aliyah*!" Though unusual, the man's logic and simple desire to be close to the *Torah* had worked for him. After-the-fact, how this is viewed in Heaven we don't know, but Reb Elazar Mendel must have understood enough to allow this man to continue as a *Levi* for so many years.

Chalukah Money

There is a Jewish custom, especially with *chassidim*, not to cut a young boy's hair until he reaches the age of three. It is customary to bring the child, usually on *Lag b'Omer*, to *a tzaddik* who can take the first snips of his hair. On the *Lag b'Omer* after his son's third birthday, the father, Reb Aharon Yosef, took him to the *beis medrash* of Reb Elazar Mendel. Many other *Yerushalmi* Jews were also waiting there with their children. However, unlike the preceding years, Reb Elazar Mendel abruptly demanded a hefty sum of money from every father who wanted his child's haircut. It was unusual, and no one could understand why the drastic change. Several *chassidim* paid unquestioningly, while others quietly slipped out of the *beis midrash* trying to be unnoticed.

Some weeks later, an epidemic broke out in Jerusalem that killed many children. However, every single child whose father had paid the *chalukah* money was saved. Clearly, the money had been accepted as a *pidyon*, a spiritual substitute that redeemed their lives. Sometimes, the *tzaddik* is not permitted to reveal his reasoning and it is best to follow through on his advice unquestioningly. Thankfully, most of the children were saved from the plague.

I am Already Committed

Reb Dovid'l Biderman spent *Shabbos* in Sanz and joined the *rebbe* for *Shacharis* prayers. But after a while, Reb Dovid'l unexpectedly left the shul. Noticing his departure, another *chassid* was curious enough to ask why. Reb Dovid'l explained, "When the *rebbe* recited *Nishmas*, he started stamping his feet with great strength. I felt him pulling me to become his *chassid*. However, I have already made a commitment to Reb Aharon of Karlin. Since I didn't want to insult the Sanzer Rav by refusing, I left the *shul*."

Review Those Mishnayos

It is very important for a Talmudic scholar to continually review *mishnayos*. By doing so, he is creating a solid foundation for his *Talmud* study to endure. So, every morning, after prayers, Reb Dovid'l Biderman would study eighteen chapters of *mishnayos*, thereby finishing the entire *Mishnah* once a month.

Others First

It is the practice of a *chassid* to regularly give *pidyonos* to the *rebbe*. All *pidyonos* Reb Dovid'l Biderman received from his *chassidim* would be given away to the poor. He simply refused to derive any personal benefit from them.

On one occasion, Reb Dovid'l's wife observed that their daughter's shoes were so torn that the rain and mud were seeping inside. Discreetly, she snuck some funds from her husband's *pidyon* chest and when Reb Dovid'l returned, she told him, "Today, I saw an unfortunate girl from a good family, who has no shoes because her family is so poor. So, I removed some cash from your charity box and presented it to her."

"Good," he happily responded. "That's precisely what it is for."

"And that girl," the *rebbezin* paused a bit before continuing, "was your own daughter."

His face turned pale. "What is done is done," he told her, "but you must never do that again. That money has been designated for the poor, and not for our family."

Children Just Need Love

A family in White Russia was once experiencing trouble with their son, Mordechai. He rarely wanted to study, only to play outside, where he had a tendency to get into mischief. This caused his parents tremendous anxiety.

Hearing the great R' Aharon of Karlin would be coming to their town, they booked an appointment for him to meet their son. The *rebbe* listened to the parents' story and responded to them very roughly. "I'll have a few words with him and set him straight. Leave him to me. I'll teach him how to behave." The parents, taken aback by his firm demeanor, yet still assured by his confidence, allowed him to take their son into his private room.

The *rebbe* leaned back on his couch and softly called the boy to come to him. He held out his arms and motioned for Mordechai to come nearer, breaking the boy's reluctance. Surprisingly, he simply pulled the boy close and held him against his heart for a long time. Nothing else happened but the simple gesture of love and respect. A few minutes later, they went out together to the parents. Not revealing his special method of persuasion, Reb Aharon of Karlin again spoke roughly to the parents. "I had a word with him. He'll shape up now!"

The boy did indeed alter his behavior and became a well-known *tzaddik*, R' Mordechai of Lecovitz, the founder of the Slonim dynasty. He forever told his *chassidim* that he first learned *Torah* from R' Aharon of Karlin, who taught him *Torah* from the heart.

Shabbos on Wednesday

On one occasion, Reb Yehuda Tzvi, the grandson of the great R' Chaim of Sanz, was attending a *seudas mitzvah* following a circumcision together with his grandfather. Rabbi Chaim was privileged to say some words of *Torah.* Since it was a Wednesday afternoon (and it is known from the holy Arizal that on Wednesday the light of the coming *Shabbos* can already be felt in the world), he commenced to expound on the holiness of the *shabbos.* R' Chaim became so enthusiastic, and emotionally charged, that when he finished he called out to those at the table, *"Shabbos Shalom, Shabbos Shalom!"*

R' Yehuda Tzvi developed the impression from all of this that indeed the *Shabbos* was soon to arrive. He swiftly ran home to get his special white clothes, and headed for the *mikvah,* to immerse himself in honor of the *Shabbos.* Along the way, he encountered another young man who had heard R' Chaim of Sanz speak about *Shabbos,* and he too was on his way to the *mikvah* to wash in honor of *Shabbos!* They jubilantly made their way together to the *mikvah,* but when they entered they saw that no one else was there. They then figured out that the excitement of the Sanzer Rebbe had caused them to think that *Shabbos* was about to come.

A Chassid From the Heart

R' Yisroel of Ruzhin once lodged in the town of Sanek during one of his travels.

As is usual when a *tzaddik* visits a town, everybody came out to greet him. Among those who eagerly rushed to greet Reb Yisrael were some Jews who were not adherents of the chassidic path. In fact, their intentions in visiting him were only to vent their hostility on Reb Yisrael.

They confronted him, "Tell us it is very difficult for us to understand. Our custom is to arise well before the break of dawn, to pray the morning prayer at sunrise according the custom of the *vasikin.* After we finish praying, we remain for some time in the *shul,* still wrapped in *tallis* and *tefillin.* We then learn *Chumash* and *Mishna* before we leave. Even as we put away the *tallis* and *tefillin* we learn chapters by memory from the *Tanach.* The rest of the day, we maintain fixed times when we gather for additional study in the *shul.* For this behavior, we are labeled *misnagedim?!*

You (the *chassidim*), your way is to pray the morning prayer long after the prescribed time for doing so, and immediately after the prayer, instead of dedicating your time for study, you race to set the table. You bring out cake and brandy, and you sit together drinking, eating, and singing. For this you are called *chassidim?!* It seems to me to be quite the opposite."

Reb Leib, the assistant of the Rizhiner, upon hearing these accusations could not remain silent. "I'm not surprised," he let out. "Your whole service is performed with so little heart, in such a calculated, chilly and lifeless manner, it is no wonder that you learn *mishnayos* afterwards, for that is what one learns in memory of the dead! (Mishna has the same letters as the word *neshama*, N*Sh*M*H) Not so the service of the *chassidim*. Whatever we do, no matter how much, or how little, we do with devotion, warmth and vitality. A living man needs a drink of brandy once in a while."

Ready to continue his rebuttal, the Rizhiner interrupted him. "You should realize that he is just joking. I will tell you the real reason for our way of praying and the secret of *l'chayim*.

It is well known that since the destruction of the *Bais Hamikdash* our prayer takes the place of the sacrifices that were offered there. As it is written (*Hosea* 14:3) 'The prayer of our lips shall replace the oxen of the sacrifice.' Our three daily prayers correspond to the daily burnt offerings. Just as a sacrifice was rendered invalid by undirected thoughts, so too is our prayer.

When a man stands in prayer before his Creator, the *yetzer harah* wants nothing more than to confuse him and introduce all manner of strange thoughts into his head. How is it possible to stand in prayer in the face of that? In the end, we are not successful in replacing the oxen of the sacrifices with our prayers. What did the *chassidim* find to remedy the problem, and with what to battle against the tricks of the *yetzer hara?*

After prayer, the *chassidim* sit together, raising their glasses in *l'chayim*, and pouring their hearts in blessing. 'Yankel, you should find a proper *shidduch* for your daughter,' exclaims one. 'Beryl, your business should have customers like the eyes on a potato,' exclaims another.

The *yetzer hara* regales in his victory over having confounded the prayer of a congregation of Jews. Seeing them eating and drinking, he concludes that their prayer is finished for the meantime, and he retires for the morning.

Now, it is a *halacha* in the *Shulchan Aruch*, that prayer can be said in any language that one understands. (*Orach Chaim* 62:2)

Therefore when Jews gather to say *l'chayim,* and to bless one another from the depths of their hearts, it is the real *tefillah.* It goes straight to the heart of the Master of the World."

Ready at Every Moment for Prayer

The Beis Pinchas reported the following story concerning Rabbi Moshe, the Rozvodover Rebbe. One time the Rozvodover Rebbe was attending a wedding and he began to *daven Ma'ariv* while sitting at the table. He did this without any advance preparation, which drew him some doubts from onlookers. When questioned about his behavior, he answered from the *gemara* in tractate *Beitza* (2a), about "prepared ashes". When one ritually slaughters a fowl or a wild animal, the spilled blood must be covered with soil. If the slaughtering is done on *Yom Tov,* then the soil must have been prepared before the onset of the holiday. Both opinions agree that ashes from the oven are considered "prepared".

The Rozvodover Rebbe explained that one who considers himself to be no more than "prepared ashes", is as worthless as ashes, can also burst into flames in an instant, just like the small coals in the ashes.

Such a person is always in a state of readiness for any matter of holiness and doesn't need any further preparation.

She Just Needed Some Sweetness

In Navardok, the home of the famous *yeshiva* that also bears this name, there were no dormitory facilities. Rather, the *bachurim* needed to rent rooms in town. The majority of landlords were happy to have *yeshiva* boys as tenants, since they were clean and considerate. One lady, a widow with a young son, had a huge twenty room house. Often, she was bitter, and made all sorts of trouble for the *bachurim.* Later she would even yell at them and ridicule them. At times during Friday afternoons, when the boys wished to prepare themselves for *Shabbos,* she turned off the water supply so that there was no hot water for bathing. Other times, she randomly turned off the electricity for no apparent reason. After some time, most of the boys decided it wasn't worth staying by her house and all the boys moved out. Yet one boy stayed, Yosef Geffen was his name.

One morning, as Yosef was walking home, the woman noticed him approaching and began to scream at him, "You must be crazy! How can you still stay in my house? You see that all the other boys have moved out, why do you insist on staying? Why not get out like they did?"

He answered her gently, in his sweet voice, "I stay here for your sake. I realize that you live alone, and I fear that one night you might fall, or become ill. You will call out for help, but there would be no one to hear your cries. I understand that you are only yelling at us because of your frustration at being widowed and because you struggle to support yourself."

Her demeanor instantaneously changed. She turned pale. Expecting a sharp remark from the boy, she was instead stunned by his caring remarks. She fell to her knees and begged his forgiveness. Forevermore, she never said anything but kind words to the *yeshiva bachurim*. She was no longer mean or nasty, and the boys began to move back into the house.

Yosef however, even though he continued to reside there, always slipped himself in the side door. For, whenever the landlady would see him, she would begin to apologize profusely all over again. How amazing it is when someone just takes a moment to understand the predicament of another person!

Priestly Robes

Following World War II, the Poles were determined to build a highway through an old Jewish cemetery. Having no choice, the local Jewish burial society had to remove all the bones to a new resting place. To their amazement, they recovered one body that had not decomposed! In Jewish lore, it is considered a sign of great righteousness that a body remains intact after so many years. Even more to their wonderment, the departed man was buried in the robes of a priest! Curious as to what was behind all these unusual findings, they made enquiries among the elders of the town, and this is the tale that was revealed:

Once, there was a *gabbai tzedakah* named Naftali. He was well respected in the community, and he would always dispense the funds fairly. Once, after he had amassed quite a sum of money for a dire emergency, a gentleman knocked on his door. "Naftali, please, you must help. I have nowhere else to turn," he pleaded. The man, already fraught by the expenses of a large family, had a child who was seriously ill, and the medical bills were piling up. This put the family under great financial distress and the man had just about all he could take. Naftali realizing an important mission, went out once again to collect. People helped, but not as they did the first time. It was, after all, his second visit collecting funds on the same day. When he returned home he was simply exhausted yet satisfied that he had done his best. As he took off his shoes to sit down, there was another knock on the door. It couldn't be, yet it was, another holy Jew needed his help. This time it was a man whose roof had caved in on his house. The family of 10 souls was homeless, and he had nowhere to turn. Naftali couldn't go around collecting three times in one day, yet that is exactly what he did.

Having little strength, he went directly to one of the wealthier townsfolk, the young son of a wealthy merchant, who was entertaining some of his friends at the local pub.

"Don't tell me you are collecting again", he shrieked in disbelief. They all began to ridicule Naftali mercilessly.

Suddenly, the young man had an idea that would help him entertain his friends. "Naftali, we will give you the whole amount of 20 zlotys that you require. All you have to do is to stroll through the main street of town wearing priest's robes." Sweet Naftali agreed to the embarrassing requirements, in order to get the job done. He was completely focused on the task at hand, that is, getting the money needed to save this family.

The wealthy man and his friends all walked behind him, singing and hooting. Other townspeople sighted Naftali, shouted curses, and pelted him with eggs. But he got the 20 zlotys, plus an extra 20, so he wouldn't have to go collecting again that day.

Naftali returned home a broken man. He threw the priest's robes in the back of his closet and collapsed into bed.

Later that year, the Divrei Chayim, R' Chaim of Sanz, passed by that same town. As he approached the house where Naftali lived he exclaimed, "I smell the fragrance of *Gan Eden* in this place." They visited the house and started to question Naftali. "What did you do that would cause the fragrance of *Gan Eden* to descend upon your house?" Naftali remembered the incident of the priest's robes and told the *rebbe* what had happened.

R' Chaim commanded the burial society that when Naftali's time comes, he should be buried in those same priest's robes. The angels of destruction will not dare to touch him, and so it was.

The Grandfather's Photograph

There once was a secular Jew in Israel. Though not religious, his family had *yichus* from a *Chassidic* background. His father shared the following remarkable story of his son's return to orthodoxy.

His son, a commander of a tank artillery division, had developed into a vehemently anti-religious person. He even went so far as to protest a photograph of his grandfather, which hung on the wall in his father's house. In the photograph, his grandfather was dressed in traditional *Chassidic* garb, with *peyos* and a long beard. The young soldier man found it particularly offensive. "That man is a barbarian. Take the picture down," he would shriek in disdain.

One day however, the soldier became religious! Why the complete backwards switch in attitude? "Let me tell you what happened," the father explained.

It was back in June 1967, during the Six Day War, in the Sinai Desert. The tanks were all spread out. If attacked, their plan was to regroup and fight together. Suddenly however, Egyptian tanks approached without warning. The commander quickly turned his tank around and sprinted back to the platoon. The fastest way was straight across an open stretch. Having not much time to decide, he began to turn in that direction.

Suddenly, he saw an old man *davening*, wrapped in *tallis* and *tefillin*, right smack in his path. "Doesn't that fool have any place better to pray than in the middle of the desert?" he shouted. "I'm going to run him over!" At the last minute, however, he swerved to avoid the old man. The Egyptian tank, while in hot pursuit behind him, didn't have any such tinge of sympathy. As it rumbled over the old Jew, it tripped a landmine and exploded into a fiery inferno.

When the soldier visited his father subsequently after the war, the photo was still on the wall. Although he had noticed it hundreds of times prior, the face seemed familiar to him in a strange way. He recognized that it was the same face of the old Jew who was praying in the desert.

"He saved my life. I realize that he was praying for me that I should live," explained the newly religious soldier to his father, "And I want to be like him."

Intentions

Chazal explain that Chanoch 'sewed shoes' and created spiritual *yichudim* for *Hashem*, similar to those created through wearing *tefillin*. This teaches us an important lesson. That even while going about their work, ordinary shoemakers or tailors can produce sublime spiritual repercussions, if they have proper intentions. We see from this that it isn't good enough to pass through life saying we didn't have an opportunity to think about *Hashem*.

Random Holy Thoughts

Reb Binyamin Kletzker, a prominent *chassid* of the Ba'al Hatanya, owned a log business. Once, while computing his earnings, he recorded out all the entries in the column correctly, but when he reached the total line, he unconsciously filled in the words, *Ein od milvado* – "Nothing exists apart from *Hashem*." Someone questioned him, "How can you be involved in *chassidus* while you're doing business?" He responded, "If, while I'm standing before *Hashem*, thoughts of the logs can enter my mind, then surely holy thoughts can enter my mind while I'm dealing with logs."

Simple Piety

The Chozeh of Lublin once told a simple but pious man, "I envy your piety for it is greater than mine. I am a leader, and whether I like it or not, everyone looks up to me. If *chas v'shalom* I do something wrong, everyone will say, 'The *Chozeh* did as follows.' You, on the other hand, work in the shadows. You can act in whichever way you want and yet you remain pious. It is clear that you are a truly pious person."

Too Comfortable

Reb Shmelke of Nikolsburg on one occasion met a Jew who could communicate with Elijah the prophet. Justifiably, Reb Shmelke became very excited. "If this be so," he voiced to the man, "ask Elijah why the messiah hasn't yet come?"

"I will certainly do so," the man rejoined, "and what better time to do so than when he comes to visit on *seder* night?"

After *Pesach*, Reb Shmelke encountered this Jew yet again and asked him if he had spoken to Elijah.

"Most definitely," the *Yiddala* responded.

"Well, what did he say?"

"He said the answer is to be found in the *Hagadah* – in the *Mah Nishtanah*, where it is written, 'Why is this night different from all other nights? On all other nights, we eat either sitting or reclining, but on this night, we all recline.' This means that on other nights during our other exiles, we had those among us who were alert. Who awakened us to our calling, who felt the pain and the suffering of *Am Yisrael*. They would move heaven and earth to bring about our redemption, but in our present exile, we are all reclined. We have become much too complacent and self-satisfied."

Speech is Holy

After the passing of Reb Yehuda ben Shoshan in the upper Galil, he appeared in a dream to his *talmid*, Reb Lapidos. During the dream, his face shone like the sun, like a blazing torch. The *talmid* questioned what he had done to merit such *kedushah*, and he explained that throughout his lifetime he had not spoken unnecessarily. A person's speech is similar to that of the *malachim* and one should use it for *kedushah* (ראשית חכמה שער האהבה פ"ו).

Personally Caring For the Guests

As a rather young married man, the *tzaddik* Reb Levi Yitzchok of Berditchev, dwelled in his father-in-law's home. His in-laws, who were well-to-do, often hosted numerous visitors. While visiting their home, Reb Levi Yitzchok would personally see to the needs of the guests, preparing bundles of straw for the bedding and proper linen. Noticing this, his father-in-law inquired of him why he troubled himself, when *goyim* could be paid to do these menial jobs. "Tell me," answered Reb Levi Yitzchok, "is it right to give a *goy* the privilege of doing such a holy *mitzvah*, and then to pay him to boot?"

Kind Acts are Equivalent

Hashem has taught us that all the kindness that we perform is more precious to Him than the *korbanos* that Shlomo HaMelech offered. Rabbi Yochanan ben Zakai and Rabbi Yehoshua were departing *Yerushalayim* together and passed by the destroyed *Bais Hamikdash*. Rabbi Yehoshua bemoaned the absence of a place of *kaparah* for the Jewish nation. Rabbi Yochanan comforted him, "Do not despair! For we still have equal opportunity for *kaparah* – via our acts of *gemilus chassadim*."

Pray for Opportunities to Perform Kindness

The Rayatz of Lubavitch related a personal story: "One morning, while on vacation in Alivka with my father, the Rashab, I awoke at 3:00 am sat down to learn. I noticed that my father had woken up even earlier and was busy preparing for *davening*. At 6:00 a.m., he invited me to come with him for a walk. As we were walking, he said to me, "When one rises in the morning, learns and then davens, something is accomplished, but without the opportunity of actually doing a kindness for another Jew, the day is 'dry'. One needs to *daven* to *Hashem* that He would send a Jew for whom one can do an act of kindness. Though, he should also *daven* that he not come across unworthy people." Later that day, two Jews from Rudnia came to my father to ask him a personal favor. My father called me and said, "You see, if one desires truthfully, *Hashem* helps him."

Kindness Every Day

A wealthy *chassid*, by the name of Reb Zalke Persitz, once related to the Rebbe Rayatz: "It is now 25 years since I became a *chassid!* In the year 1897, the Rashab shared with me some advice during my *yechidus*. He said, 'Just as a Jew must put on *tefillin* every day, he must spend fifteen minutes a day thinking about himself, and whom he can help *b'ruchnius* or even *b'gashmius*.' I inquired of the *rebbe*, 'how is this possible?' To which he responded, 'For this one must have a *mashpiah*,' and the *rebbe* suggested Reb Zalman Arsher. Henceforth, each day, I would record in a diary the act of kindness I had done that day, and on a day when I could not find someone with whom to do a favor, I would go to shul and spend time with Reb Zalman."

Pride is the Tzaddik's Enemy

Towards the culmination of one of Reb Dovid of Lelov's regular fasts, he was traveling on the road and felt a rare extreme thirst. It felt unbearable to simply ignore. Unexpectedly, noticing a spring of cool bubbling water in his path, his thirst intensified to the point that he felt coerced to break his fast and drink. Before a *tzaddik* completes an act, he ponders the plus and minus of what he is about to do. There he stood still, reflecting for a moment to consider the matter further, and thereby he found an inner strength to squelch the thirst. Continuing his way, he sensed such a great rush of joy, having prospered in subjugating his *yetzer harah*! Soon however, another thought came to mind. He began thinking to himself, that joy is not coming from the *yetzer tov* after all, but rather from the *yetzer harah*. He's trying to persuade me to be filled with pride!" In order to avoid falling into the trap, Reb Dovid returned to the spring and drank his fill. So important was it to him to avoid all forms of pride.

Simple Fear of Hashem

The Rayatz of Lubavitch related an important reminder for us about true fear of *Hashem*. "In earlier times, even the simplest *yidden* had *yiras shamayim* that you could feel. Before making a *brachah* they would carefully clean their hands. I remember playing in the garden as a child, when I heard a gardener say the *brachah, shehakol* with such feeling that I trembled. This was not a profound *yiras shamayim* that grows out of deep understanding, but rather a simple fear of Heaven. This expressed itself not only in abstaining from wrong and doing good, but also in a *hiddur mitzvah*."

Fear of the King

Once, while attending a party, a certain baron portrayed to his fellow noblemen the awesome atmosphere in the king's palace. He described how all the servants, in their various ranks, stood in dread before the king. As he continued speaking, the baron went into great details about the king. He was so overwhelmed that he fainted. When they succeeded in waking him, they questioned: "Were you ever in the king's palace, and did you experience this fear?"

"No," he responded, "I was never even near the palace."

"How then do you know all these details?" the baron was asked.

They probed further. "My brother was a guard for the king," the baron clarified. So too, by contemplating the greatness of *Hashem* and His kingdom, a person will be filled with awe, even though he has never actually seen Him.

Don't Plan During Shabbos

Without any warning, one of the well-to-do *Yidden*, residing in *Yerushalayim*, began rapidly losing his riches. This continued until he reached dire straits. One of his acquaintances went to Reb Shlomo'le of Zvil requesting a *yeshuah*. Surprisingly, the *tzaddik* said, "Had this man not thought about his business matters on *Shabbos* and *Yom Tov*, he would not have lost his possessions." When the former wealthy *Yid* heard what the *tzaddik* had said, he confessed, "The *rebbe* is correct. I used to do business with Arab dealers on *motzei Shabbos* and *motzei Yom Tov* and would therefore plan these transactions during the afternoon hours on the holy days." From that day forward, the *Yid* stopped planning, and his financial situation improved drastically.

What Good is it if I don't Have True Fear of Hashem?

The *tzaddik* Reb Mendel, of Rimanov, began learning in the *yeshiva* of the Nodah Biyehuda. Once, after many years of learning,

89

he was studying from the Rif's *sefarim*. Abruptly, his thoughts began to bother him, "Look, I have already finished *Shas Bavli* and *Yerushami* with all the *rishonim*, and I remember it all clearly, but of what good is it if I have not merited to truly stand in awe of *Hashem* in its true sense!" Reb Mendel began to cry profusely and he fell asleep on the *sefer* he was currently studying. As he was in slumber, the Rif appeared to him in his dream and spoke: "You should know that our *neshamos* are connected and therefore your awakening came as you learned my *sefer*. If you want to reach true awe of *Hashem* go to the city of Lizhenzsk, to Reb Elimelech. There you will merit the true service of *Hashem*." And so, it came to be that Reb Mendel eventually became a *chassid* and then a chassidic *rebbe* in his own right.

A Plain Neshamah

When Reb Michel of Zlotchov came to the Ba'al Shem Tov, the *rebbe* gave orders to show him the utmost respect, declaring, "You should know that this man is the son of the holy Reb Yitzchak of Drohvitch. His father did not have a lofty *neshamah*. In fact, almost no one the generation possessed such a plain *neshamah*. Only with his tireless efforts did he elevate it to a level akin to that of Rabbi Shimon Bar Yochai."

An Honest Yid

There was once a certain *Yid* who was so occupied with his business throughout the entire week that he had only *Shabbos*, to devote himself to studying *Torah*. He felt so defective about this that he asked a *chacham*, "What can I do that will be equivalent to all other *mitzvos* and will bring me to *Olam Habah*?" The *chacham* responded, "Since you are a businessman, make sure to deal honestly with both *Yidden* and *Goyim*. Tilt the scale to benefit your customer, and always do your business dealings with a smile." The *chacham* then closed by saying, "If you do so, may my portion in *Olam Habah* be like yours!"

Honest Even For a Loss

The *amorah*, Rav Safra had an item that he was selling. Once while he was reciting *kriyas shemah*, a client approached him and offered to purchase it for a certain price. Since Rav Safra failed to respond, the man presumed that he just wanted more money. So, he offered a higher figure then his previous offer. When Rav Safra finally finished his prayers, he sold the item to the man at the original price. Why, because in his mind he had already agreed to the first offer and it would not be honest to take a penny more.

Non-Kosher Middos

We know that non-*kosher* food effects the mind, but what about other things? We live in a generation where right and wrong, in business dealings, can take a backseat in order to help one's own financial growth. Once, Reb Menachem Mendel of Rimanov was asked why we find that pure young children who *daven*, and learn with fervor, later leave that path entirely. He went on to explain that this is often a result of being fed food bought with dishonest money, which then breeds negative *middos* and desires just like non-*kosher* food.

No Time For it

Reb Yosef Rozin, the Rogatchover Gaon, served as *rav* for the *chassidim* in Dvinsk. The *gaon*, accounted for every second of his time. Although he possessed other talents, he decided to not get involved in anything other than *Torah*. At one point, the Rogatchover asked a *bachur* to translate for him a letter written in Russian. After doing as instructed, the *bachur* turned to his instructor in surprise, "*Rabbi*, why don't you learn the language? You could surely do it in half an hour!" The Rogatchover grinned and said happily, "It would take me half that time, but from where should I take fifteen minutes?"

I Too Would Like a Share

Once, while the builders were erecting a *succah* outside the house of the great *chassid* and *rav* of Babroisk, Reb Hillel Paritcher, the aging *rav* himself appeared. Grabbing one of the hammers, he joined the effort by knocking nails into the walls. The men pleaded with him, *"Rebbe*, we do not need your assistance. You can rest assured that we will build for you a *kosher succah."* The *tzaddik* answered, "You should know that the four walls of the *succah* correspond to the four letters of *Hashem's* holy Name. I too want a share in this."

Too Strong of a Business Mind

There were two business partners who once visited the Ba'al Hatanya for assistance in resolving their argument. The *rebbe* skimmed their contract, finding exactly where the solution could be found. Quite impressed and satisfied, the two departed. It wasn't long though that they returned with a different argument. The same thing repeated itself, the *rebbe* investigated their contract and found the needed clause to resolve the matter quickly. After a few more repetitions of this occurrence, the *rebbe* inquired about the author of their contract to see what was behind this. It was Reb Boruch Mordechai. On his next visit to the Ba'al Hatanya, the *rebbe* reprimanded him, "Your head's too engrossed in business if you are able to think of every situation that can crop up between *shutfim*. Use more of this energy for *Torah,"* he explained to him, "and make your business of secondary importance instead."

Teshuva is Simple

A *yid* once expressed to the *tzaddik* Reb Yisroel of Ruzhin, "*Rebbe*, I have committed *aveiros* and I want to do *teshuvah."* When the *tzaddik* asked him why he didn't do *teshuvah* already, the simple Jew responded that he didn't know how. "Well, how did you know how to do the *aveirah*?" questioned the *Tzaddik.* "I just did it," the man said. "So, do the same now. Just do *teshuvah* and the accounting will follow." the *tzaddik* clarified.

Tehillim With the Boys

The fourth *rebbe* of Lubavitch, the Maharash, would venture out for fresh air in the countryside for a few days in the summer. While there, he often stopped in one of the forests for some solitude.

Once there, he would sit on the ground and recite *tehillim* tearfully on behalf of *Klal Yisrael*. On his way, he would bypass a certain Jewish-owned inn, having never before entered. Unexpectedly, however, this time he did enter, finding two young boys unsupervised. The *rebbe* requested them to bring him a *tehillim* and together the boys chanted the *pasukim*, repeating each word after him. When the mother came back home, needless to say, she was happy and somewhat surprised to find the *rebbe* with her children. The sweet tunes to which they were all reciting *tehillim* brought her to tears. After a while, the *rebbe* got up to depart. As he approached the door, he turned around, took the *tehillim*, and continued with the children some more. Sometime later, he blessed them all and went his way. Hours passed, night fell, but the father failed to return home as usual. The mother did her best to assure her children that he would return shortly, but she was quite fearful something was amiss. Finally, in the middle of the night, there was a sudden knock on the door. Hearing her husband's voice, the mother hurriedly opened it, but after her husband entered he fell to the floor in a faint. After he recovered slightly, he disclosed his day's experience: "I had gone to collect an old debt from one of the gentile farmers. He invited me into the barn, claiming he'd pay his debt with grain. Instead he locked the door, tied me up, and threatened to kill me. I pleaded with him, saying that I would completely absolve him of his debts, but he wasn't swayed. Searching for his axe, he left the barn and tied the door from the outside. Realizing that my end was near, I began to recite *vidui*. At that moment, his wife passed the barn, heard my cries, and entered. I begged her to set me free. At first, she wouldn't hear of it, fearful that her husband would kill her. At last she gave in, untied me, directed me to the best escape route, and quickly returned to the field. When the *goy* returned he was fuming and chased after me. I had anticipated this, so I was hiding in the tall grass along the road. The *goy* came so close to me that I could smell his whiskey stench. *Baruch Hashem*, he passed me as I waited a while to be sure he would not see me as I hurried home." Hearing his tale, the woman exclaimed "Now I understand why the *rebbe* stopped by today and said *Tehillim* twice with the boys. Once, so you would be set free, and again so that the farmer should not find you. Blessed be *Hashem*, Who always works miracles, for us!"

Taller for Shabbos

Rabbi Pinchas Levi Horowitz was described by the Tosafos Yom Tov as "wise in *Torah* and worldly matters", and as "head of the four lands in Poland." Every Friday afternoon, when donning his *shabbos* finery, he seemed to grow a foot taller, only returning to his regular height at the end of *shabbos*.

Clouds Move Away

Reb Shmuel Shmelke's son was Reb Meir, who was *rabbi* of the towns of Belchov, Zlotchov and Tiktin. He was widely recognized as a holy man, great in *Torah* and charitable deeds, immersed in *Torah* study day and night. Upon one *motzei Yom Kippur*, Reb Meir and his *beis din* went out to sanctify the new moon. Not being a clear night for reciting the prayers, the sky was cloudy and murky. Reb Meir cried out, "How brazen is the sky! Meir and his *beis din* are waiting!" Instantaneously the wind blew the clouds apart and they could see the moon. Then they began the prayer of *kiddush levanah*.

The Fiery Preacher

Reb Shmuel Shmelke's son was Reb Meir, Rabbi of Belchov, Zlotchov and Tiktin. He was an exceedingly humble man. One time, a traveling preacher delivered a fiery sermon to the habitants of Tiktin, rebuking them for their sins. Reb Meir personally broke down in tears. "Why embarrass me in public?" he complained. "If you have to rebuke me, why not do it in private?" The preacher was surprised. He clarified that his words had been meant only for the simple townspeople, but Reb Meir was unappeased.

"All of our townspeople are *tzaddikim*. You couldn't mean them. Who could have sinned except me?"

You Reached For a Pillow

Reb Shmuel Shmelke Horowitz of Nikolsburg and Reb Pinchas Horowitz of Frankfurt, the Ba'al Hafla'ah's mother said of them: "I have two sons; one never says *Birkas Hamazon* because he hardly eats, and the other never recites the bedside *kriyas Shemah* because he doesn't sleep."

The two brothers put every ounce of their strength into their study of *Torah*. They once struggled over a difficult *Torah* topic for more than a day. The Hafla'ah, about to collapse from exhaustion, grabbed a pillow and lay down.

"Why are you sleeping?" his brother called to him. "Get up and learn!"

"I am too tired," replied the Hafla'ah. "I have no more strength."

"You had enough strength to reach for a pillow. You should have used that strength to learn a few more lines!" Reb Shmelke called out.

Another time, they studied together for two and a half days straight, without sleep, in the attic of the *beis medrash*. The Hafla'ah went downstairs to get a certain book they required. After a long delay, Reb Shmelke went to look for him, and found him collapsed on the stairs from exhaustion. Reb Shmelke woke him up saying, "My dear brother, if we sleep now, what will we do in the grave?"

A Full Day of Torah

Reb Shmelke's *yeshiva* in Reitshval attracted the loftiest *Torah* minds, including the Kozhnitzer Maggid, Reb Levi Yitzchok of Berditchev, Reb Menachem Mendel of Rimanov, and Reb Mordechai Banet. Their everyday schedule encompassed fourteen hours of *Torah* study, four hours of prayer, a half hour for rest (during which Reb Shmelke would teach *Chovos Halevavos*), a half hour for meals, four hours for sleeping, and one hour open for the public. Although they had such a strenuous schedule, the study periods often extended beyond the planned *z'manim*.

The intensity of their devotion to *Torah* study was outstanding. The Hafla'ah wrote, "When I visited my brother's *yeshiva* in Reitshvl, I saw young men tie their *peyos* to the rafters with strings. If they started to fall over in sleep, the pain would jerk them awake."

Time To Get a Pillow

One scholar of that generation, Rav Meir Karinsnofler, *av beis din* of Brodt and author of *Yad Hameir*, once transcribed his attempts as a youth to enter Reb Shmelke's *yeshiva*. He journeyed to Reitshval, where Reb Shmelke cautioned him, "The main condition for studying here is that you never willingly go to sleep during the week." Rav Meir agreed, and for two full days he sat and studied at the *yeshiva*. By the third day he could barely keep his eyes open when Reb Shmelke began to deliver a complex lesson in *gemara*. Suddenly he required a specific book from his private study and sent Meir to fetch it. Wearily, as he continued searching through the bookshelf, he noticed the *rebbe's* bed right beside it. He could no longer resist, and sleep overpowered him. He grabbed a pillow and sank to the floor.

After some time, Reb Shmelke directed another student to search for the book and for Reb Meir. The *bachur* returned and reported that Meir was sleeping on the floor.

"Does he have a pillow?" Reb Shmelke questioned. "Yes," the student replied.

"Too bad. If he didn't have a pillow, I would let him sleep because he had no other choice. But if he had time to put a pillow under his head, he went to sleep willingly. Go wake him up."

Meir awoke, realized what had happened, asked Reb Shmelke for his blessing and went his way. He wasn't physically and emotionally ready for Reb Shmelke's *yeshiva*.

Rekindling the Light

When Reb Shmelke had to sleep, he would lay his head on a jar of cold water and wedge a lit candle between his fingers. If he overslept, the candle would slowly burn down and wake him. By this method, he would learn throughout the night. He used to tell over, "If a person holds the precious diamond of *Torah* in his hand, should he willingly throw it away?"

One evening, as Reb Shmelke napped, the wind blew out his candle. Upon awakening, he sprinted out to the porch to get a light from a passerby. Out of nowhere, a hand appeared out of the darkness and rekindled the candle. Reb Shmelke quickly returned to his studies, not thinking too much about it. In the morning, he comprehended that his study was on the second floor, well beyond human reach! Realizing what must have happened, he fasted for several days afterwards to atone for troubling Eliyahu *hanavi* to come to his aid.

When Reb Yehoshua Heshel, the Apter Rav, heard this story, he sighed. "Those are the sins Reb Shmelke has to repent for, having troubled Eliyahu *hanavi* to help him study *Torah*. Where does that leave us!"

Even a Little Pride

When word reached Reitshval about Reb Dov Ber, the great Maggid of Mezritch, Reb Shmelke and his brother, the Hafla'ah, decided to pay him a visit. "Why do *tzaddikim*, like you, have to travel so far to see me?" the *Maggid* enquired of them on their first encounter. When they lingered in silence, not knowing the correct reply, he continued, "So I will tell you. A *chassid* can rise at midnight, to pray and study until dawn, with great concentration. Then he can recite the morning prayers with such holiness that he ascends through all the supernal worlds. But, if after his prayers he feels even the slightest bit of pride, Heaven takes all his prayers and *Torah*, crumples them up into a ball, and throws them into the abyss!"

The two brothers, stirred to their depths, responded, "The *rebbe's* right we did not need to travel to meet him. We needed to crawl to him on our hands and knees!"

"What did you learn in Mezritch?" his comrades asked Reb Shmelke upon his homecoming to Reitshval. "Before I met the *Maggid*," he said, "I fasted so my body could bear my soul. In Mezritch, I learned how the soul can bear the body!"

Pawning His Wife's Ring

One day, a poor man came to Rabbi Shmelke's home collecting for food. There was no cash in the house, but the *rebbe* knew the man was desperate. So, R' Shmelke searched through his wife's drawer, and found a beautiful ring. He promptly gave it to the beggar hoping it would be plenty to help him. When his wife returned home, she screamed, "How dare you give that ring, it was

97

worth fifty dollars! Now go and run after the beggar!" Which Reb Shmelke promptly did, whispering in the beggar's ear. "I have just learned that the ring I gave you is worth fifty dollars. Make sure you don't get less for it."

The Song of the Sea

Upon arriving in *shul* to pray, Reb Shmelke was joined by a sizeable group of *chassidim*. They did not fail to notice the unusual liveliness of the *rebbe's* prayers. They also felt energized by the *rebbe's* powerful spirit, and that day's *Shacharis* had a special quality. The tale is told that on that day, when the *rebbe* reached the *shiras ha-yam*, the Song at the Sea, the entire congregation was swept away by a powerful vision of the Jews crossing the Sea of Reeds with Moshe Rabbeinu at their helm. So much so that R' Shmelke actually picked up his *bekishe* as he stepped into the raging waters. The *chassidim* too followed suit, so deep was the revelation with the *rebbe*. This was not pretentiousness. That day they accurately satisfied the obligation of our sages that, each person should imagine that he himself was redeemed from Egypt.

The Importance of Saying Amen Properly

Rabbi Chaim of Volozhin was meticulous in reciting a blessing, only when someone else was present to answer *amen*. On one occasion, while studying into the wee hours of the night, he sensed he needed to drink a cup of water. He looked around but there was no one to answer *amen* to his blessing. Just then, one of the elite students of his *yeshiva* came to the study hall to ask him to explain a complicated commentary of Tosfos on the Talmudic tractate. Rabbi Chaim elucidated the Tosfos, and then he said the blessing on the water. The student answered *amen*, and Rabbi Chaim thanked him, whereupon the student went about the rest of his day.

The following day, Rabbi Chaim mentioned to the young man, "Thank you once again for answering *amen*. I was so thirsty last night. I wouldn't have been able to continue learning without your help."

The student, confused, said he didn't understand what the *rebbe* was referring to. He had slept the entire night and did not visit him.

Rabbi Chaim of Volozhin then understood that it was Eliyahu *hanavi* who had appeared to him, in the appearance of his student, to assist him with his resolution to say a blessing only when someone was present to answer *amen*.

Amen v' Amen

Before making a blessing, Rebbe Shmelke of Nikolsburg always made sure that someone would be close by to answer *amen*. He explained that when one recites a blessing it creates an angel, but the angel isn't complete unless somebody answers *amen* to it. However, there was simply no Jew in sight to answer *amen*.

One time, when Rebbe Shmelke was traveling, he descended from the carriage in order to relieve himself. Afterwards, he was required to make the after blessing of *asher yatzar*, but there was no Jew in sight to answer *amen*. Suddenly, he noticed two people coming his way. He recited the blessing and they promptly answered *amen*, with *kavanah*. Then they simply vanished.

Rebbe Shmelke guessed that these two 'men' were actually the angels Raphael and Gabriel. They were sent down from heaven, enabling him to complete the blessing properly.

Shortly after, he fell asleep in the carriage and it was revealed to him that he had assumed correctly. The two "men" were indeed the angels Raphael and Gabriel, and his interpretation was also correct.

Traveling with Eliyahu Hanavi

There is a tradition that if a person were too fast for 40 days in a row, he might have a revelation of Eliyahu *hanavi*. Reb Yehoshua ben Levi, on one occasion, fasted for several days and *davened* that he be granted this revelation. His request was granted and Eliyahu appeared to him, saying, "Whatever you desire, I will fulfill."

Reb Yehoshua requested to be allowed to accompany him, to observe what he did and to learn from him. "But you won't be able to handle the sights that you will encounter," Eliyahu cautioned him. Reb Yehoshua insisted on his wish. Eliyahu agreed, with one condition, Reb Yehoshua could not question anything Eliyahu did, or he would not be able to continue. Together they headed out until they reached a small, dilapidated cottage. There they were eagerly welcomed by a poor man and his wife. They treated their guests with the best sleeping accommodations and meals that they could manage.

In the morning, after the prophet and the sage got ready to leave, Eliyahu *hanavi* stood beside the couple's only cow and prayed that it should die. Reb Yehoshua gasped in astonishment. Was this the reward for the unfortunate couple's graciousness – to kill their only source of livelihood?! Nevertheless, recalling the condition, and wanting to continue with Eliyahu *hanavi*, Reb Yehoshua kept silent. After traveling until evening time, they finally arrived at the home of a well-to-do man, who neither greeted them nor invited them to share any crumb of his bountiful provisions. The next day, as they were leaving, Eliyahu *hanavi* prayed for a wall of the wealthy man's home that had collapsed be reconstructed. Once more Reb Yehoshua was astonished but kept quiet. However, similar experiences continued to happen until he could contain himself no longer. He asked Eliyahu for an explanation of all the confusing circumstances he had witnessed. Eliyahu then revealed to him the decree from Above that their gracious hostess was to die that very day, and he had prayed that their cow be taken instead. This was in fact a tremendous kindness to the couple. As for the wall of the greedy man, it was positioned above a precious treasure that he would have uncovered, now it would remain hidden from his eyes. Thus, not everything was as it appeared to be. That was the last time Reb Yehoshua could accompany *Eliyahu*.

Just Wait, Have Some Faith

Two *chassidim* were, on one occasion traveling to the Ba'al Shem Tov, when they found themselves slowed down behind the local landowner's wagon. It was taking its time rambling down the road and they didn't have all day to follow behind him. One concerned *chassid* turned to the other: "If we're going to continue along at this pace, it's highly unlikely that we'll reach Mezhibuzh before *Shabbos.*"

"Don't worry," his friend assured him with faithfulness, "I have no doubt that whatever *Hashem* does is for the good." As they continued talking, they reached a very narrow passageway that was blocked by a broken-down wagon carrying jugs of milk. The landowner hopped down and arranged for the driver to move the jugs to another wagon and move away the wagon that was obstructing the road. His orders were heeded, and the path was cleared. Soon they all continued their way. The landowner moved his wagon to the side of the road so the wagon carrying the *chassidim* could easily pass by. "Now I see that you were right," remarked the *chassid* to his companion. "If the landowner had not been in front of us, we would have had to wait until the milk wagon was fixed. The driver would not have moved the jugs for us as he did for the landowner!"

Lifeless Torah study

The Ba'al Shem Tov, on one occasion, opened the door of a *yeshiva* but declined to enter. "What's wrong?" his *chassidim* queried. "I cannot enter because the room is full of *Torah*." Isn't that a good thing?" they asked.

"No," he replied. "It is full because the *Torah* learned here lacked the fear and love needed to ascend to Heaven, and it lies lifeless on the ground."

Where is the Milk

Once a wealthy local philanthropist invited Reb Shmelke to his home. As they sat down and talked, a maid fetched them a pot of coffee. Reb Shmelke requested some milk, and his host pointed to a small pitcher that was already on the table. After a few moments, Reb Shmelke once again asked for the milk. His host realized that something was amiss and went into the kitchen to investigate the matter further. He discovered that today the gentile maid had milked the cow without the required Jewish supervision, thus the milk was not *chalav yisrael*.

"The *rebbe's* correct," he remarked as he returned to Reb Shmelke. "This milk is forbidden. But why didn't the *rebbe* just simply say so? Why did he have to ask where it was?"

"I honestly did not see it," Reb Shmelke explained. "The *Shulchan Aruch* states that 'Milk that is milked by a gentile, which a Jew does not see, is forbidden.' This implies that milk milked by a gentile, a Jew does not even see, and I didn't!"

Parting the Ice

Reb Shmelke was summoned to Vienna on some matter. He and Reb Moshe Leib Sasover traveled there on a chilly winter day. It was common during the middle of the winter that the Danube River, on the outskirts of Vienna, was frozen. However, it was the only way to cross into Vienna. Inquiring who would take them across, none of the ferrymen would agree, for they feared the large blocks of ice floating downstream. One ferryman finally agreed. While embarking, Reb Shmelke stood at the prow of the boat and sang the *shiras hayam*, while Reb Moshe Leib sang the bass accompaniment. The large masses of ice instantly parted and allowed the small boat to pass through.

Coffee or Snuff

Reb Dovid'l's father-in-law dedicated his entire *Shabbos* to *Hashem*. He would not sleep at all, from the beginning of *Shabbos* until its departure. As soon as his Friday night meal was completed, he retired to his study and began an extensive program of study. First, he studied the weekly *parsha* with all its commentaries. Then he studied the *Zohar* and other kabbalistic works. He learned books from all four levels of *Torah* study: *pshat, remez, drush, and sod.* The entire evening, he could be found leaning over his books, studying by the light of a tiny lantern. His voice echoed in the stillness of the house. A coffee urn stood at arm's length on the burner, and close to him on the table was a small box of snuff. Every so often, he would pour himself a cup of coffee and with his other hand take a pinch of snuff. So deep in concentration was he, that he never took his eyes off the book in front of him while preparing the coffee. During one *Shabbos* night, he could easily drink twenty-four cups of coffee, and inhale an entire box of snuff!

Reb Pinchas of Brod, each *erev Shabbos*, would purchase the coffee and snuff himself from the same spice merchant. As soon as the *rabbi* arrived at his store, the merchant would pour a scoop of roasted coffee beans into a small hand-grinder and, from there, into a paper bag. Into a separate paper bag, he would pour freshly ground snuff. "*L'chovod Shabbos kodesh*," Reb Pinchas would say, as he paid for them.

"One time, when my father-in-law was too elderly and weak to walk to the spice shop, I volunteered to go for him," Reb Dovid'l said. "The merchant prepared for me his usual requirements into the two small bags but, when I returned home, I inadvertently poured the snuff into the coffee urn and the coffee into the snuff box. Since their colors were similar, I did not notice my mistake.

"That evening, following the meal, my father-in-law spent the entire night learning, as usual, drinking his coffee and smelling his snuff, without noticing anything. After *Shabbos* was completed, he questioned me, 'What happened to the snuff this week? It had a funny smell.'

"I rushed to his study and examined the remnant of the snuff, it smelled like coffee! I then opened the coffee urn, and it reeked of tobacco!

"That my father-in-law drank the tobacco without noticing a difference didn't surprise me. There are times that a person becomes so immersed in his studies that he doesn't notice anything, as the *Talmud* says [about Rabbi Yehoshua ben Levi and Rava] ... I believe that my father-in-law was on that *madrega*. However, what I couldn't understand is that, if he was completely absorbed in his studies, why did he indeed notice the change in snuff?

"Finally, the answer became clear to me. Coffee is something you drink, it is a physical pleasure. However, smell is a spiritual experience. My father-in-law was completely above the physical. Therefore, he couldn't detect the coffee's change but the snuff, being a completely spiritual experience, was something he clearly noticed."

Learning Torah All Day

Reb Pinchas Dovid HaLevi Horowitz and his wife moved to Tzfat, to live near his father-in-law.

Reb Meir Shochet, one of Pinchas Dovid's many *chavrusos* in Tzfat, described the young *tzaddik's* daily schedule. Reb Pinchas

Dovid had six different study partners and learned three hours with each, for a sum of eighteen hours a day! During the remaining six hours, he would *daven* and see to his daily requirements. Nevertheless, since his fiery prayers were so extensive, they made up the better part of the six hours, allotting him almost no time to sleep.

Reb Meir, Reb Pinchas Dovid's first study partner, would connect with him early each morning, before dawn. Due to Reb Pinchas Dovid's agenda lasting late into the night, he requested Reb Meir to politely knock on his bedroom window on his journey to the *beis midrash*. "But I never once woke him up," Reb Meir reported. "He was always waiting for me!"

Reb Pinchas Dovid also studied *Torah* with Reb Moshe Liers, later the *rav* of Tiberias, and with Reb Mordechai of Slonim, the forthcoming Slonimer Rebbe.

He also learned at *Yeshivas bar Yochai*, in Meron, under Rabbi Yaakov Eliezer Fraiser. He was in the habit of leaving Tzfat, on Sunday, and would return home the following Friday. His study partner during that time was Rabbi Meir Yechezkel Holzberg, the future *rav* of Rosh Pinna in the Galil. Together, they would learn for eighteen hours straight, without wasting a single minute.

Frozen in Fear

Each year on *Lag B'Omer*, the *yahrtzeit* of Rebbe Shimon bar Yochai, Reb Pinchas Dovid HaLevi Horowitz would travel to Meron. One year an enraged Arab raised his hand to strike him, only to have it literally freeze in midair. The Arab began trembling in fear because he could not move his arm and begged Reb Pinchas Dovid for forgiveness. Only after he forgave him was the assailant able to lower his hand.

Pure Simple Words

Although the Maggid of Chernobyl was a *gaon* in *Torah* with a brilliant mind, he still knew when to act with complete simplicity, as can be seen from the following story:

The *chassidim* of R' Motel of Chernobyl noticed him standing by the window moving his lips. They moved closer to hear what he was saying, imagining he was meditating on some deep kabbalistic prayer. However, they were shocked by what they heard. He was simply saying, "*Ribono Shel Olam*, the maid that helps my wife wants to quit, but my wife really needs her assistance, so please make the maid change her mind." The *chassidim* couldn't believe what they heard, and asked the *rebbe* why he, the prodigious *gaon*, was praying like a simple person, requesting of *Hashem* for such a simple thing. Replied the *Maggid* in all simplicity: "Who else should I ask?"

The Wedding Invitation

A grandchild of Reb Levi Yitzchok of Berditchev was engaged to wed a grandchild of the Ba'al Hatanya. After Reb Levi Yitzchok was shown a draft of the invitation, indicating that the *chassunah* was scheduled to take place in Zhlobin, he ripped it up. Then he instructed that the wording be changed to read, "The *chassunah* will take place *im yirtze Hashem* in *Yerushalayim Ir Hakodesh*, in the *Bais Hamikdosh*, may it be speedily rebuilt. However, if (*chas veshalom*) *Moshiach tzidkeinu* will not yet be here, then the *chassunah* will take place in Zhlobin."

Who are We

The Chasam Sofer had a tradition to often learn from the *sefer*, Megaleh Amukos. One time, a notable guest came to visit, and he noticed the Chasam Sofer learning the *sefer*. He expressed his appreciation and own interest for the *sefer*. "Let me tell you a story," told the Chasam Sofer. "The Russian czar would often stroll in the royal gardens of Petersburg and, according to the law, no visitors were allowed in the gardens during this time. Once, a simple *melamed* from a small town visited the garden, ignorant of the above-mentioned regulation. As he was taking a stroll, he met up with none other than the czar himself! The czar sternly inquired, 'Who are you and what do you do?' The *Yid*, unaware to whom he was speaking, mentioned his name, origin, and source of income. Then he rebutted, 'And what is your occupation, sir?'

'I?' snickered the czar. 'Why, I am the czar who rules over the entire Russian empire!' The *melamed* shrugged his shoulders. 'Alright, this too is an effective way of making a living…' So too," the Chasam Sofer concluded, "Who are we to give an opinion about this holy *sefer*?"

How to Yearn For Moshiach

Tzaddikim living during the time of the *tzaddik* Reb Moshe Teitelbaum, the Yismach Moshe, would declare that he was a *gilgul* of Yirmeyahu *hanavi*, who prophesied the *churban* of the first *Beis Hamikdash*. He would constantly weep about this lengthy *golus*, especially throughout the Three Weeks, and he yearned daily for *Moshiach*. Whenever he perceived some noises in the street, he would scurry towards the window: his immediate thoughts were, "Had *Moshiach* just arrived?" Beside his bed lay his best *Shabbos* attire, readily prepared. Each night before retiring to sleep he would warn his *shammes* to awaken him the moment the *shofar* of *Moshiach* was heard. Once he received a letter informing him that on a specific date his beloved son-in-law would be arriving for a visit. Everyone in the household prepared excitedly for his arrival. When the special day arrived, the visitor was nowhere to be seen. This made the family restless. What could possibly have delayed him, they wondered? Meanwhile, the Yismach Moshe was seated in his room, engrossed in his *seforim,* while some family members waited outside impatiently. Suddenly, when a carriage suddenly appeared on the horizon, the *rebbe's shammes* ran indoors to bring him the good news: "*Rebbe*, he has arrived!"

The *rebbe* leaped up from his chair, clothed himself in his fine *Shabbos* clothes and *shtreimel*. Then he ran outside towards the approaching carriage. Unfortunately, and fortunately, he saw none other than his son-in-law stepping down from the carriage. In shock, he was unable to bear the pain and fell to the ground in a faint. When he came to, his family heard him moaning to himself, "Oy! It's not him... He hasn't yet arrived..."

If He Doesn't Come By Tomorrow

As a *yeshiva bachur* in Pressburg, Reb Yosef Chaim Sonnenfeld, later the *rav* of *Yerushalayim*, recalled once overhearing a woman asking her friend what she had made that day for supper. "Squash," came the reply. "And for tomorrow?" The woman questioned further. The other lady responded back in haste, "*Chas veshalom!* Don't speak like that. If, *chas veshalom, Moshiach* doesn't come by tomorrow, then I'll make lentils..."

Generous to His Wife and Others

The Arizal would make it a habit to learn six explanations in the literal meaning of a *halachah*, corresponding to the six days of the week. Afterwards, he would learn the *halachah* according to *the kabbalah*, corresponding to *Shabbos*. Regarding his personal needs he was sparing, wearing rather simple clothes, and was in the habit to limit his food intake, not eating much. Nevertheless, for his wife he provided generously, even when he could not really afford to do so. Regarding giving *tzedakah*, and other *mitzvos*, he also maintained a very generous standard. He was extremely careful not to talk in *shul*, even if it was not the time for *davening*. He would not even talk words of *mussar* in *shul*, lest he stumble into speaking mundanely.

I am Dust and Ashes

The *gaon* Reb Chaim Rapaport, the *rav* of the city of Lvov, was a prodigious adversary of the Ba'al Shem Tov. One time, while he was studying alone in the *beis medrash*, a man entered. When Reb Chaim questioned who he was, he replied, "I am mere dust and ashes (*afar va'eifer*)."

The guest then questioned, "And who are you?" Reb Chaim rejoined, "I, too, am mere dust and ashes."

"If so," rebutted the unnamed guest, "why should there be *machlokes*, between us?" Reb Chaim then understood that this guest was none other than the Ba'al Shem Tov. From that day forward, he became attached to him, and later fulfilled many significant missions on his behalf.

Making Peace Between Friends

Chazal instruct us, "Be one of the students of Aharon Hakohen, loving peace and pursuing peace..." It was told about Aharon that when he heard of two friends who were quarreling, he

107

would approach one of them and say, "My son! Do you know what your friend is doing? He is beating his chest in anguish right now and tearing out his hair. He is saying, 'How can I look my friend in the face? I am so embarrassed to have sinned against him!' Upon hearing this, the listener would of course forgive his friend in his heart. Aharon would then visit the other man and duplicate the process. Later, when the two met, they would embrace and kiss each other. So, it was that when Aharon passed away, eighty thousand Aharons, born as a result of his peacemaking, attended his funeral, and all *Bnei Yisrael* mourned Aharon for thirty days.

Making Peace

One Friday night, Rabbi Meir's *shiur* for women finished far later than usual. When one of his listeners eventually returned home, she found her husband so irritated that he would not allow her in the door. He said she could only return if she would go and spit in the speaker's face! What should she do, she wondered? Her friends encouraged her to visit Rabbi Meir for advice and they accompanied her. As they neared his home, he sensed the dilemma with *ruach hakodesh*. Acting as if his eye was hurting and had dust stuck in his pupils, he greeted the ladies, "Can one of you please spit in my eye to heal it?" The woman grasped the opportunity and soon returned home having fulfilled her husband's wishes. After they left, his *talmidim* questioned, "Rabbi! Isn't this a disgrace to the *Torah*?" Rabbi Meir replied, "My honor cannot be greater than the honor of *Hashem*, Who allowed his Name to be erased, in order to make peace between husband and wife."

Chazal teach, "If the *mizbeiach* is to be treated with reverence for its peacemaking between the *Yidden* and *Hashem*, how much more certainly will an individual who brings peace between husband and wife, or between families or communities, be spared punishment and be granted a long life!" (ספרא קדושים כ, תנחומא יתרו יז)

Helping Couples is a Mitzvah

When the Ba'al Hatanya lived in the town of Mohilev, he had to sacrifice time from his learning in order to bring peace between a struggling couple. His *chavrusah* complained: "True, *Chazal* teach us that bringing peace between husband and wife is so special a *mitzvah* that one is rewarded for it in this world and the next – but don't they also infer that the study of *Torah* is equivalent to all of the *mitzvos*?" In response, the Ba'al Hatanya indicated that the *Mishnah* places "bringing peace" next to *Talmud Torah* – in order to teach us that each of those two *mitzvos* is equal to all the others. Therefore, bringing peace can be as important as *Torah* learning.

I Will Rock the Infant, You Go Back and Learn

Once time, R' Zusha went into the kitchen and requested some food. The cook replied that she had nothing to give him and would have to go buy some groceries to prepare him a meal.

However, she certainly could not leave her infant unattended. R' Zusha gladly offered to watch the baby until she returned.

R' Zusha sat by the baby's crib, studying the *sefer* of the Shelah *hakodesh*. When the baby began crying, R' Zusha put the book down and began rocking the cradle. The holy Shelah came down from *Gan Eden* and told him, "I will rock the cradle. You go back to learning my *sefer*."

Only the Truth

The Chofetz Chaim was obligated to appear as a character witness in a trial. When he declined to be sworn in because he would never take an oath, the attorney told the judge that he may well waive the oath, because the Chofetz Chaim is incapable of deviating from the truth.

He then told the judge the following story. Once, the Chofetz Chaim noticed a thief walking off with his candlesticks. He promptly exclaimed in a loud voice that he abandoned his ownership of the candlesticks so that the thief would not be committing theft. "A man like that does not lie," the attorney remarked.

The judge retorted, "Do you expect me to believe that story?"

The attorney answered, "Your honor, they do not tell stories like that about you or me."

There is No Way of Escaping It

During the self-imposed exile that he accepted along with his brother, the *tzaddik* R' Elimelech of Lizhenzsk, they lodged at a motel where the only available sleeping arrangements were on two shelves. That night, the villagers entered and indulged in a lot of drinking. After they became tipsy, they danced around in a circle, and every time they danced past the two sleeping men, one of the party goers would purposely land a heavy blow on R' Zusha.

R' Elimelech suggested, "My brother, why should you absorb all the beatings? Let us change places."

After they switched places and the tipsy batterer was soon to land another blow, a comrade told him, "Why are you always hitting the one on the bottom shelf? Why don't you hit the one on the top shelf, too? Which he promptly did.

R' Zusha whispered to his brother, "You see, Melech, if it is *bashert* for Zusha to be beaten, there is no way of escaping it."

I Have Never Had Anything Bad Happen To Me

A *chassid* requested the Maggid of Mezeritch to clarify the Talmudic ruling that a person should thank *Hashem* for the bad things that happen to him just as he would for the good things (*Brachos* 54a). How can that be expected of a person? The *maggid* instructed him, "Go over to the man who is sweeping the floor and ask him."

When the man stated to R. Zusha that he could not understand the passage in the *Talmud*, R' Zusha commented, "I cannot help you. I am not a Talmudic scholar." The man insisted that the *Maggid* had directed him to pose his question only to him. R' Zusha responded again, "How could I possibly answer your question? I have never had anything bad happen to me." The man glanced at R' Zusha, whose tattered clothes testified to his abject poverty, and he had the answer to his question.

Hashem said, Hashem said

Rav Yisrael of Rhizin explained that R' Zusha did not transmit many of the teachings of the Maggid of Mezeritch. This is because, when the *Maggid* began his discourse, "And *Hashem* said," R' Zusha was so overcome by an ecstatic fervor that he began shouting uncontrollably, "*Hashem* said, *Hashem* said!" This caused such a commotion that he had to be escorted out of the room. Even after being led out, he stood in the hall, beating his hands against the wall and shouting, "*Hashem* said!" Thus, he never stayed through a complete discourse from the *Maggid.* "However," R' Yisrael stated, "If a person listens in the spirit of truth and speaks in the spirit of truth, he can uplift and redeem the entire world with a single word. That was R' Zusha's greatness."

In Your Majesty's Presence

R' Zusha of Anipoli was actually the one who brought his brother R' Elimelech of Lizhenzsk to the Maggid of Mezeritch. R' Elimelech was a great Talmudic scholar, and asked his brother, "Zusha, why do you spend so much time in prayer? Why don't you spend more time studying *Torah?*"

Rav Zusha responded with a parable:

Once there was a simple person, a woodcutter, who developed an intense desire to see the king. From village to village he wandered, finally arriving at the capital city. When he found his way to the palace, he just stood outside the palace gate, hoping to get a glimpse of the king when he left the palace.

After some days, the guard at the palace gate questioned him as to why he was standing there. The woodcutter communicated to him that this was his only hope of getting a glimpse of the king. Seeing the man's sincerity, he permitted him to enter the palace courtyard, where he again took up a vigil.

Before long, one of the officers in the courtyard also asked him what he was doing there. Being impressed with the man's sincerity, he decided to take him into the palace. He was eventually approved to heat the palace by making the fires. The word spread to the king that he had a citizen who was totally devoted, and the king summoned him to the throne room.

"I see that you are sincerely devoted to me," the king remarked. "Do you have any wish that I can grant you?"

The man answered in faithfulness, "I know that I am a simple person, and do not deserve to be in your majesty's presence, but perhaps I could have a room with a window overlooking the entrance to the throne room, so that I could see your majesty come and go." The king granted his wish.

Once, the king's son committed an offense for which he was exiled from the palace for a year. He longed to return to the palace, and upon meeting the woodcutter requested his woodsman's clothes. "That way I will be able to get into your room and see my father."

The woodsman answered, "No, that is not fitting for you. You are the prince, and you deserve to be in the king's presence constantly. All you must do is ask your father's forgiveness and pledge not to repeat your errant behavior, and you will be warmly received. I have no claim to be in the king's presence. All I can do is watch him from my little room."

"You see, Elimelech, you are a great *Torah* scholar. Your vast knowledge of the *Torah* endears you to *Hashem*, and you are like a prince in the royal court. But I am unlearned and have no claim to be permitted in the King's presence. If I do not pray fervently and stoke the fires of heaven with prayer, how shall I ever get close to the King?"

What Have You Done

Just by looking at a person, R' Zusha was able to perceive the wrongdoings he had committed. Speaking to himself, he would then utter, "Zusha, Zusha! What is it with you that you have been so sinful? Just look at what you have done!" Then he would go on to rebuke himself for all the wrongdoings the other person had done. Invariably, this would penetrate to the person's heart and result in his doing *teshuvah*. What is important to understand is that most *tzaddikim* perceive only the good in people. The only reason R' Zusha saw more was because he personally felt connected to every Jew and he truly felt their sins were his. In some way he too sinned, even if it was on a lower scale.

It's important to support your Rabbi

Rav Zushe of Hanipoli was a great and humble man. One resident recognized Rav Zushe's exceptional *madregah* and began to assist him financially.

The villager arrived to visit Rav Zushe in his home, but Rav Zushe was away. He had departed to visit his *rabbi*, the Maggid of Mezritch. This caused the villager to reflect a bit about his assistance to Rav Zushe. He thought, "Why should I spend my money on the student? I might as well forget about him and go support the *rabbi*."

After a few weeks passed, the villager noticed that his financial situation was slowly deteriorating. Uncertain as to why there was a recent turn of events, the villager resolved to pay a visit to Rav Zusha to ask for advice.

After listening to the entire story, Rav Zushe summarized his problem: "You decided to scrutinize if I was worthy of your support and decided that my *rabbi* was worthier than I. *Hashem* treated you the same and scrutinized you. He then decided that someone else, was worthier than you, to have your wealth."

The villager immediately began again to support his local *rav*, Rav Zushe, and soon his fortune returned to him as before.

Reb Zusha Feels the Pain

Rav Zusha was certainly one of the most interesting figures in the Chassidic movement. He was a genius but not in the normal way of other *tzaddikim*. He was renowned for his humility and love of humanity, especially Jews.

One time, he was sitting in his back-yard learning from a *Torah* book when wild-looking fellow pounded on the gate. After just a few moments, he busted through the front door waving a blank piece of paper and a pen. He stood there with his eyes enraged. His roughness and insensitivity could be seen all over his face as he stood before the *rebbe*.

"You are Rabbi Zusha right? The famed Rabbi Zusha that everyone talks about?"

When the *rebbe* didn't protest, the man continued speaking.

"Here, here, take this paper and write me a letter that I'm free of sin and I can have my dress coat. Here!" He placed a paper and pen on the table and just glared at the *rebbe,* waiting impatiently.

Reb Zusha gazed at the man blankly in the eyes, trying to discern if he was sane.

Then he said, "I don't understand. What connection is there between my letter and your coat? Please take a seat and explain yourself." The *rebbe* motioned for him to pull up a chair, but the man ignored his request. He just looked exasperatedly at the sky, then returned his glance towards the *rebbe* and said, "*Rabbi,* the *chassidim* took my dress coat. They said that because I had done a certain sin I wasn't fit to wear it and they'd only give it back if you wrote me a letter. And I want it returned. I mean, the fact is I could have done a lot of sins... so what? Does that give them permission to take my clothes? So, what if I..." And he proceeded to specify what sin he had done.

"Did you really do such a sin?" The *rebbe* questioned, even though it seemed obvious he had.

"What difference does it make what I did!" he blunted. "Just write the letter! Just write! Nu?!"

"But, my friend, please listen." The *rebbe* said in his sweet voice. "How can I write a letter saying that you didn't sin when it could be that you did! That would be a lie."

"Alright! So, don't write that I didn't sin. I forgot to tell you that they said you could write that I repented. They said, the *rebbe* must either write that I didn't sin or that I repented. Okay? So just write that I did *teshuvah* and I'll go get my coat." He said with no more patience.

"But I can't write that either." The *rebbe* pleaded. "I have never lied in my life. So, I couldn't write that unless I know you really did repent and that you regret it so much you won't do it again."

"Arrrgggggghhh!!" The man bellowed in frustration. "Why are you making so many problems? It's just a coat!! If I went to the priest and begged him he would have mercy and write. Is the holy *rabbi* more stone hearted and cruel than the priest?! Maybe I should just go to the priest and finished!!!!"

Upon hearing these words, Reb Zusha seemed to go berserk. He stood and, holding his head in his hands yelled out, "OY!!" His eyes filled with tears, his heart broken, and he dizzily started to wobble like a drunk. "Oy! I caused a Jew to say such a thing! How? How? OY!!"

He became so disoriented that he stumbled about his yard until he tripped and fell into the sewage ditch that was in the corner. Onlookers heard the commotion and saw the *rebbe* laying there. Without delay they pulled him out of the muck and brought him into his house. They helped him clean up and change his clothes and laid him down. He moaned and groaned and went to rest in his bed for a while to recover.

In the meantime, when the commotion began the visitor unobtrusively hid behind some bushes and silently watched what was happening.

Recognizing that this was all about him, he was sure the *rebbe* was just putting on some show to get rid of him and he'd be lucky to ever see his coat again. But after a few seconds he realized it wasn't an act and he intently began to watch as events unfolded.

"Aha!" He pondered to himself. "I get it! This *rabbi* is probably such a fanatic that he can't stand the mention of other religions. That's why he's going crazy!!"

But soon after, he began to have his doubts about that theory as well. Could it be that Reb Zusha was completely serious?

He could hardly believe it. It HAD to be a show! It just had to be!! No one was that serious about G-d!!!

However, when they brought the *rebbe* into his house it suddenly dawned on him that the *rebbe* was pained about him. Up until now he had completely missed the point of Judaism and of life.

Reb Zusha was in a trauma because for a Jew to leave Judaism is like leaving life itself! He was pained because he caused a Jew to consider spiritual suicide! Not just life in the afterworld but life right NOW!!

The visitor started to feel remorse. Holding his head in his hands and with tears streaming down his face, he ran to the house, entered Rav Zusha's room and found him sitting on his bed swaying from side to side with red eyes pouring tears, saying "Why?? Why??"

"*Rabbi!*" He stated, "*Rabbi...* I'm sorry! I'm sorry for what I said! Please forgive me!"

"Ahh, the coat!" Replied the *rebbe* "Here, bring the paper I'll write that you repented. Please forgive me for what I did."

"No! *Rebbe!* No!" He exclaimed, also weeping in tears. "Forget the coat, I don't even want the coat!! All I want is for *Hashem* to forgive me for all the senseless mistakes I've made. Please *rebbe*! Tell me how!"

The *rebbe* just slid down from the bed, sat on the floor and beckoned the man over, "Come, sit next to me and we will both ask for forgiveness. I'm sure that together we'll draw *Hashem's* mercy."

Together they sat and wept over their mistakes for almost a half an hour. When the man left, he became a totally different person.

Imagination and Vision

Rav Mendel of Rimanov used to say that only on the eve of *Shabbos*, after immersing in the waters of the *mikvah*, could he understand a small piece of the *sefer Noam Elimelech*, written by Reb Eliemelch. (*Ohel Elimelech* 92)

Long before Rav Mendel Rimanover was revealed as a *tzaddik* and *rebbe* possessing *ruach hakodesh*, he appeared at Reb Elimelech's table as just another *chassid*, a regular devoted follower.

There was one *Shabbos* that the Rimanover was sitting with all the other *chassidim* when the *shamash* brought in the *rebbe's* soup and placed it before him. The *rebbe* took the bowl of soup in his hands, overturned it, and spilled its contents onto the table. Suddenly gripped with fear, the Rimanover shouted, "*Oy! Rebbe*! Surely, they will put us all in jail. You must stop immediately!"

The other guests almost burst into laughter after hearing such strange comments coming from Reb Mendel. However, to give honor to their host, the *rebbe*, they restrained themselves. Reb Elimelech replied to his worried *chassid*, Reb Mendel, "Relax, my son, we are all safe. We are all here right now." The other *chassidim* were astonished at the *rebbe's* remarks as all the events and words spoken seemed out of place. So, Reb Elimelech went on to clarify what had transpired that led him and Reb Mendel to say what they did.

"A high-ranking government administrator was determined to pass a harsh decree against the Jews. He had tried many times prior but was unsuccessful. He intended to write out charges and have the king stamp and seal them with his ring. Today he tried again, determined that this time nobody would interfere with carrying out his wicked plan. He was ready to use sand to blot the ink and dry it when I overturned my soup bowl. The official became temporarily confused and he picked up the inkwell instead of the sand and proceeded to spill ink all over the accusatory letter he had just written! This young man," the *rebbe* said, resolving the mystery of Reb Mendel, "could witness what I did, but only by divesting himself fully from the physical world. So, he forgot that we were in fact here in this room. He actually imagined that I had used my physical hand and overturned the inkwell. This frightened him, and in his terror, he called out for fear that we would be arrested for my actions." Now everyone understood what lofty a level of *ruach hakodesh* this young man could perceive. (*Ohel Elimelech* 185)

Now you can better understand why people light a candle and say "*le'illui nishmas haRav hatzaddik* Menachem Mendel ben Reb Yosef zt"l."

Then they pray to *Hashem* in his merit. This is because he said before he passed away, "he would do a favor for anyone who lights a candle for his *neshamah*."

Seeing the Separation of Light and Darkness

One time, Reb Mendel of Rimanov told his teacher, Reb Elimelech, that he actually saw the angel who removes the light before the darkness and the darkness before the light (as described in the first blessing of the *Maariv* service). The *rebbe*, Reb Elimelech retorted, "But I have already seen this angel in my youth!" (*Ohel Elimelech* 156)

Trembling From Fear of Hashem

Reb Menachem Mendel of Rimanov once told Reb Moshe Chaim Efraim of Sudilkov, the author of *Degel Machaneh Efraim* and grandson of the Ba'al Shem Tov:

"My holy master and teacher Reb Elimelech of Lizhenzsk would meditate on the awe and fear of *Hashem* each day. When he would do this, his whole body would shake and tremble. Fear and trepidation would literally seize him. Everyone present could observe him trembling violently from the sheer awe of *Hashem* and the majesty of the Almighty. All his tendons and ligaments could be seen, thick and taut as ropes; his face would alter its color and even his vein below his ear would begin bulging. I received a tradition from my *rebbe* that there is a vein located below the ear that only

117

trembles from fear of the day of death. With my *rebbe*, this vein trembled daily from his great fear of *Hashem*." (*Eser Tzachtzachos 2; Seder Doros HeChadash*, part 4)

Travel To the Rebbe

Once, during his youth, Reb Menachem Mendel of Rimanov was studying in the *beis medrash* under Rav Daniel Yaffe in Berlin. He would learn the works of Rav Alfas (the Rif) on the *Talmud*, diligently. His soul thirsted longingly for self-perfection.

He learned so much in one sitting that his tongue stuck to his palate. He had a spark inside that caused him to pray deep in his heart, and he cried to *Hashem* to enlighten him. He prayed and prayed, until he had no strength left and fell into a deep sleep. In his dreams, he saw the Rif himself! The Rif showed him an image of Reb Elimelech of Lizhenzsk and instructed him to travel to the *rebbe*, for there he would succeed in attaining his goal. (*Ohel Elimelech* 183)

Handing Over His Splendor

When Reb Elimelech left this world on the twenty-first of Adar in the year 5547 (1787), he lay his hands upon his students and gave to them of his own splendor. To the holy Reb Yaakov Yitzchak, the Chozeh of Lublin, he gave the light and power of his eyes. To the holy Rebbe Yisrael, the Maggid of Koznitz, he gave the power of his heart. To the holy Rebbe Mendel of Pristik (later known as the Rimanover), he gave the spirit of his mind, and to the holy Rebbe Avraham Yehoshua Heshel of Apt, he gave his power of speech. And after his passing, the land shined with their glory. (*Ohel Elimelech* 186)

Handing Over the Leadership

There is a story told of Reb Elimelech's brother, Reb Zusha of Hanipoli. After Reb Elimelech passed away, his disciples approached his brother Reb Zusha of Hanipoli and requested of him to be their new leader.

Reb Zusha declined their request. This is what he told them:

"The *Torah* is eternal and alludes to everything that has happened and will happen for all generations. The *posuk* 'And a river went forth from Eden to water the garden, and from there it split into four paths' (*Bereshis* 2:10) alludes to the paths of *chassidus* and great *tzaddikim* of our times. '*Eden*' alludes to our holy master the Ba'al Shem Tov. The river is his disciple, the holy Mezritcher Maggid, and the garden refers to my brother, Reb Elimelech. The *Torah* flows as water from the Ba'al Shem Tov by way of the Mezritcher Maggid to Reb Elimelech. From there it separates into four paths, and they are the holy *rebbe* the Chozeh of Lublin, the holy Koznitzer Maggid, the holy Reb Mendel Rimanover, and the holy *Ohev Yisrael* the Apta Rav. You need no *rebbe* other than them."

Hashem Provides for All Flesh

The *rebbe* from Komarna related that he heard from his father-in-law the *tzaddik*, Avraham Mordechai of Pintshov, that Reb Zusha, in his impoverishment, served as a *shamash* in Ostra. He would regularly fast for two or three days in a row. Then he would request one of the residents for some bread to satisfy his hunger. Once Reb Zusha thought to himself that it is a lack of faith in *Hashem* to go begging and asking for bread. So, he resolved to trust in *Hashem* alone, and *Hashem* will send him his food and sustenance. So, this time, after fasting for three consecutive days, he was weak and on the verge of death, however no one presented him any food. This caused a great uproar in the heavens, since no one was found worthy of the *mitzvah* of sustaining so lofty a soul and giving Reb Zusha something to eat! Though there were many worthy, upright individuals in that town, no one was of the caliber worthy of the *mitzvah* of supporting Reb Zusha. *Hashem* then fashioned a miracle, so that two nipple-like openings opened in Reb Zusha's mouth. From one, would come forth milk, and from the other honey. For three consecutive months Reb Zusha was nourished from these miraculous openings alone. After another three months went by, somebody finally approached Reb Zusha and offered him 6 *groshen* to buy bread. From that point on, the miracle stopped, and the openings closed.

The lion's den

The Ba'al Shem Tov was heard to say that Reb Chaim was befitting to be *moshiach*, in his generation. The Ohr Hachaim declined to benefit from his *Torah* learning and therefore supported himself by being a goldsmith. Each day he would only spend the minimal time working, as per his employer's needs, and would then quickly return to his learning. Once a king placed a large order of jewelry to be made for his daughter's wedding. A deadline was given for its completion, but because at that time the Ohr Hachaim was not desperate for money, he refused to take off learning time just to have the order ready for a certain date. When the king heard his lack of respect, he flew into a rage and ordered that the Ohr Hachaim be thrown into a den full of lions and other wild beasts.

When the time arrived for the verdict to be carried out, the entire *yiddishe* community escorted the *tzaddik*, all the while weeping and lamenting over the terrible decree. The gentiles also showed up, however, they came to watch the show, excited to see a Jew being eaten alive by hungry, ferocious animals. However, the Ohr Hachaim remained calm, placing complete *emunah* in *Hashem*. While being led away, he kept encouraging the *Yidden* that *Hashem* would definitely assist during this hour of need. All the items he carried with him were his *tallis, tefillin,* and some *seforim*. The crowds watched as the Ohr Hachaim was lowered down into the cage. After several days passed, the caretaker of the royal garden went to clean up whatever remains were left of the body. However, to his utter astonishment, he observed the *tzaddik* wrapped in his *tallis* and *tefillin,* totally engrossed in his learning. The usually ferocious lions were sitting around him like children in front of a teacher! The caretaker hurried to let the king know, and his royal highness rushed out to see this extraordinary sight. Immediately, the king commanded that Reb Chaim be taken out and he then proclaimed with deep feeling, "Now I know that there is a G-d among the Jews!"

Whatever a Yid Hears is a Lesson

During one of his weekly trips from the city of Datshe back to the town of Lubavitch, where the Rashab would visit his mother and receive guests for *yechidus*, Shaul the wagon driver stopped nearby a well. He wanted his horses to drink so they would continue their journey faster. When they finished, he whipped their backs and shouted, "Fools! Do you think I've given you water for your own benefit, so that the hay you've eaten should be tastier?! Not at all! I've given you water so that you'll have more strength and desire to *shlep* the wagon!" Hearing this, the *rebbe* reflected in deep thought for some time and then remarked, "The Ba'al Shem Tov taught that whatever a *Yid* hears and sees is a lesson in *avodas Hashem*. A *Yid* must remember that he is given his physical needs in order to have the strength to pull the *ruchniyus'dike* wagon, through *Torah* and *avodah*. One must not err and think that what really counts is the hay, just for us to enjoy."

One Minute

During a visit of the Rashab of Lubavitch to Germany, some locals accompanied him to the railway station and one of them remarked that the train would be leaving in another minute. The *rebbe* responded with some *mussar*, "In one minute one can do *teshuvah.*"

Unable to Hear Praise

The Ba'al Shem Tov was once sitting and praising Reb Nachman Horedenker, while Reb Nachman himself was sitting at the end of the table. He was bent over, trying to hear the words of his *rebbe*. To the astonishment of the other *chassidim*, it was a wonder he could be so eager to hear praise about himself. The Ba'al Shem Tov clarified to them: "Reb Nachman asked *Hashem* for a gift not to hear those things that he should not hear, and therefore, he actually did not hear anything that I spoke concerning his greatness. It was for this very reason that he tried to bend over, for he thought that I was saying words of *Torah* and he wanted to hear. The proof to all this is that when I say *Torah*, he does not need to bend over."

Forgo Everything for One Amen, Yehei Shmei Rabba

One day, the Ba'al Hatanya spoke out to the *chassidim* and remarked, "In *Gan Eden*, they appreciate the preciousness of *Olam Hazeh*. The *malachim* would forgo everything for one *'amen, yehei shmei rabba'*, said by a *Yid* with all his might (recited during *Kaddish*), with complete concentration and total involvement in those words." He said no more that time, yet with it he kindled such a burning enthusiasm in his listeners that throughout the entire following year, *amen, yehei shmei rabba* was said with fire.

Amen After Siberia

Reb Zalman Leib Astulin was a Russian *chassid* who was exiled for many years in a Siberian prison. He wasn't the only one. There were many Jews sent to Siberia due to discrimination. Being cut off from other *Yidden*, he was powerless to *daven* in a *minyan*, to hear *Kaddish*, or even answer *amen* to a *brachah*. Years later, he left the Soviet Union and traveled to *Eretz Yisrael* where he met his brother-in-law, Reb Yankele Galinsky, in Bnei Brak. It was a delighted reunion. The following morning, Reb Yankele took Reb Zalman Leib to a nearby *shul* to *daven*. After *Shacharis*, Reb Yankele proceeded home and Reb Zalman Leib stayed on. Time passed and although the *shul* was nearby, which meant that he could not possibly have lost his way, Reb Zalman Leib failed to return home. After some time, Reb Yankele went to *shul* and found his brother-in-law standing there, supported by his crutches, his face radiating with joy. "Why are you still here?" Reb Yankele questioned. "You probably finished *davening* long ago, so come home and eat something."

"I just can't leave!" answered Reb Zalman Leib. "After my *minyan* finished, another one began, and then another, and each one offers me a chance to say *amen, yehei shmei rabba* and *kedushah* again and again. *Hashem* finally gave me this precious opportunity – and I should give it up just for breakfast?"

I Replaced it With a Good Tongue

The king of Spain respected R. Shmuel Hanagid so favorably that he appointed the brilliant and righteous *talmud chacham* as his second in command. However, that brought some jealousy to other officials. One such officer had a store inside the palace and he envied the sage more than the others. Whenever he saw him passing by, he would go outside and curse him, but Reb Shmuel never paid much attention. Once, while Reb Shmuel was going for a stroll with the king, the *goy* came out and, as usual, cursed him. The king became furious and demanded Reb Shmuel to cut off the storeowner's evil tongue. After some investigation, Reb Shmuel discovered that this *goy* was a pauper, so he began sending him money regularly to help him, and this softened his heart very much. After a while, when Reb Shmuel once again took a walk with the king, the *goy* came out and this time began praising him. The king, who had not heard clearly what the *goy* had shouted, queried Reb Shmuel why he had not followed his original instructions to cut off that man's tongue. "I did do as you commanded," answered Reb Shmuel. "I cut off his bad tongue and replaced it with a good tongue."

They are Still Yidden

The *chassid*, Reb Berke Chein, was imprisoned and exiled in Soviet Russia because they caught him spreading *Yiddishkeit* in the underground Lubavitch network, defying Stalin's religious suppression. Unfortunately, the informers who had him arrested were fellow *Yidden*, who had unfortunately been influenced by Communist beliefs and created the *Yevsektsia*, a "*yiddishe*" branch of the NKVD. Quite some years later, at a *farbrengen*, Reb Berke shared his story with a group of *chassidim*, and upon mentioning the share of those *Yidden* in his imprisonment, he muttered to himself, "May *Hashem* forgive them! They are still *Yidden*." After all the hurt, he still bore no grudge against them for all the pain they had caused him.

A Night With the Shechinah

The two *tzaddikim*, Reb Shlomo Alkabetz and Rav Yosef Caro, spent the night of *Shavuos* together in Tzfas. R. Shlomo Alkabetz shared the events of that night: "The Beis Yosef and I decided to stay awake on the night of *Shavuos* and read passages of the *Torah*." These passages are the basis of what later became the *Tikkun Leil Shavuos*. "After *chatzos*, as we reached the section of *mishnayos*, a sweet voice was heard aloud from the mouth of the Beis Yosef. We fell on our faces from sheer fright. The voice grew ever louder, until even the neighbors were able hear it, though they were unable to understand it. The voice, having been created by the *mishnah* we had learned, told us of the pain suffered by the *Shechinah* [in exile], and the significant impact our learning this night had, silencing all the *malachim* and piercing all the heavens. It then spoke of our great *zechus* by staying awake this night, and the greater effect it would have had with a *minyan*. The voice then encouraged us to continue learning throughout the night, not wasting even a moment. Finally, the *Shechinah* instructed us to stand up and say *baruch shem...* out loud, as is done on *Yom Kippur*. We wept profusely from the intensity of our experience and the pain of the *Shechinah*.

"The next morning, we met three *chachamim* in the *mikvah*, and we related to them what had occurred the previous night. They were understandably distressed, and we all resolved to gather again the following night, this time with a *minyan*. That night, because of our joy at having a minyan, the voice of the *Shechinah* began speaking as soon as we started reading the *Aseres Hadibros of Devarim*. The voice praised our attainment, told us of the *ruchnius'dike* fire surrounding the house, and then directed us to say *baruch shem*. As the time of *chatzos* drew near, the *Shechinah* spoke again and told us that for hundreds of years no such revelations had occurred."

The Shaloh Hakadosh quoting this story from the *ksav yad* of Reb Shlomo Alkabetz concludes: "It is apparent from his writing that there was much more that he was not allowed to reveal. From this story, we must learn how important it is to conduct ourselves with special *kedushah* on this night."

Temporary Loss of Vision

The *davening* of the *tzaddik*, Reb Yitzchok Aizik of Ziditchov, was always animated by the fear of *Hashem*. This was even more pronounced when he read the *Aseres Hadibros*. The entire *shul* would stand in awe and tremble as they listened. His *neshamah* seemed in danger of leaving his body. One time, while he was reading the *Torah* on *Shavuos*, one of his *chassidim* became so swept up that he lost his vision throughout the recital of *kriyas haTorah*. Alarmed, he conveyed it to the *rebbe*, who enlightened him that this occurred because they had been passing through the "darkness, cloud and fog" which surrounded *Har Sinai*. Soon after, his vision returned.

A Simple Question

A simple wagon driver would transport people from Homil to Paritch for his *parnasa*. Once he approached Reb Aizik with a question. "I am a *Kohen*. Am I permitted to take a divorcee in my wagon?" (He obviously knew that a *Kohen* may not "take" a divorcee for marriage, but he was concerned that he may be prohibited from taking such a woman in his wagon as well). Reb Aizik went to a box of *seforim* in order not to embarrass him for asking such a simple question. He pulled out a *sefer Smeh*, looked inside for fifteen minutes, and then turned to the man and said, "Where? To Paritch? Yes, you may." The Rayatz of Lubavitch noted, "Fifteen minutes was a lot for Reb Aizik. During that time, he could have been learning in depth, but since one may not laugh at an *am ha'aretz* who asks a question (to avoid causing him to stumble on another occasion), Reb Aizik therefore disregarded his time."

He Left in Fire

On the day that Rabbi Shimon bar Yochai was preparing to leave this world, he instructed his son Reb Elazar and the *talmidim* who were gathered around him, "This is an auspicious time. I am now going to reveal holy secrets that I have on no occasion yet disclosed. This way, I will arrive in *Olam Haba* without reason for embarrassment. I see that today is a distinctive day, for *Hashem* and all the *tzaddikim* are rejoicing in my celebration (*hillulah*)." He charged his *talmid*, Rabbi Abba, to write down what he was about to say, Rabbi Elazor to repeat it, and the other *talmidim* to pay attention carefully. Rebbe Shimon then revealed to them the section of *Zohar* known as *Idra Zuta*.

At that moment, the *kedushah* of Rabbi Shimon was so intense that none of the *talmidim* could gaze upon him, and throughout the day a fire surrounded the house, concealing everyone else at an awed distance. Rabbi Abba recollected: "While I was in midst of writing, and Rabbi Shimon was in the middle of quoting a *posuk*, he stopped at the word *chaim*. I paused, wanting to continue, but could not raise my head to see why he had stopped, for I was unable to glance upon the bright light that he radiated. Suddenly, I heard a voice call out a *posuk* that included the word '*chaim*', and then another voice called out another *posuk*. I fell to the ground and wept. When the fire diminished and the light faded away, I saw that the great luminary, Rabbi Shimon, had passed away. He was lying on his right side, a smile beaming from his face." Soon residents of nearby Tzipori came to take Rashbi to bury him in their village. However, the inhabitants of Meron sent them away. Meanwhile the bed, which was now outside the house, raised itself in the air, while a fire burned brightly in front of it. A voice rang out, "Come and gather for the *hillulah* of Rabbi Shimon!" When they entered the cave in which he would be buried, another voice was heard, coming from within. "This man shakes up the world and all its kingdoms. Many adversaries in *shamayim* are silenced because of his merit. *Hashem* glories in him daily. Fortunate is his portion, both above and below!"

The Elderly Man in White

Reb Elazor Azkari, recognized by the title of his *sefer* as the Ba'al Hachareidim, was a *shammes* in a *beis medrash* in Tzfas. He was widely regarded as a simple person. No one fathomed his true *kedushah* and *Torah* scholarship. During *Lag BaOmer* one year, he traveled to the *kever* of Rashbi in Meron. While there, he encountered the Arizal and his *talmidim* and danced with them for a long time. He also danced with an elderly gentleman who was clothed in white. The elderly man was dancing with intense joy. Soon after, the Arizal seized hold of the elderly man's hands and danced with him for a while, and then danced with the Ba'al Hachareidim as well. Upon leaving the *kever*, the *talmidim* questioned the Arizal, "You must have danced with the elderly man because he is a great person, but why did you dance with the *shammes*? It is true that he is a *yerei shamayim*, but is it suitable for you to dance with him?" The Arizal laughed and remarked, "If the Rashbi danced with him, isn't it an honor for me to dance with him as well?"

Good Soup for Chickens

When the Pri Megadim would eat his meals by his father-in-law, his mother-in-law did not fancy him hurrying down his food and hurrying back to his *seforim*. In order to try to get him to stay longer and chew slower, she would prepare scrumptious, delectable foods for him. However, she soon realized that her efforts were for naught. He did not really care for food altogether, and so she decided that he was a *batlan*, who was oblivious to these things.

One time, she decided to test him. For the daytime meal, she served everyone a bowl of soup, but to him she served a bowl of cloudy water. The Pri Megadim held his cool and did not comment. He simply drank the entire serving. His father in-law chuckled, "Ha! What do you say, good chicken soup?!"

"Yes indeed," the Pri Megadim replied. "Good soup for chickens."

Take a Lesson From Honor

The Chacham Tzvi had a tradition of going through old letters that had been sent to him. He would read over the many titles of honor that people bestowed on him. Upon being questioned as to his intent when doing this, he explained, "If the world writes such titles, this obligates me to be so much more careful with my deeds, for what would the world think if such a person sinned?" He then gave a *perush* to the *posuk*: "*Adam bikar*" - if a person has honor, "*velo yavin*" – and he does not take a lesson from it, "*nimshal kabehaimos nidmu*" – he is surely likened to an animal.

Wealth Can Blur Your Vision

A poor *chassid* once grew rich and proudly took all the credit to himself for his change of fortune. He, now respected no one, not even the *tzaddik* Reb Michel of Zlotchov. Once, as he passed Reb Michel's house, he acted as if he did not notice the *tzaddik*. Reb Michel however, went out towards him and invited him inside. Once inside, he led him to the window, and pointed to what was happening outside. "What do you see through the window?" Reb Michel asked the rich man. "I see people coming and going," he replied. Then he brought him in front of a mirror. Reb Michel questioned the man again as to what he saw. "A reflection of me," he answered. Reb Michel then explained, "What's the difference between the two? The glass of the window is not coated with silver, so a person can see others. A mirror, by contrast, does have a silver backing. That's what limits his vision so that he can see only himself."

The Mitzvah of Ahavas Yisroel

During the *seudah* of his *bar mitzvah*, the Rayatz of Lubavitch inquired of his father the Rashab. "Why is *hareini mekabel* mentioned before *davening*?" The Rashab explained that before we request of *Hashem* our needs during prayer, it is appropriate that we cause Him *nachas*. A father's greatest *nachas* is when he sees his children act with *achdus* and express their brotherly love for one other. When the Rayatz repeated this, he further added that the *mitzvah* of *Ahavas Yisrael* entails not only giving food, loans, or a place to sleep. It is a *mitzvah* in which a person should invest his entire essence, to the extent that the other person's needs become more important than his own needs. Indeed, elder *chassidim* would often say, "Love yourself as much as you love others."

I Sleep Quickly

The holy Sanzer Rebbe would not sleep very much, just a few hours a day. When questioned how this does not affect his health, he replied, "They say that I grasp things very quickly. What takes someone else a long time to comprehend, takes me a short while. The same is with sleep. I sleep quickly."

Bedikas Chametz Until the Morning

One year, in advance of *bedikas chametz*, the Rayatz of Lubavitch said, "One must check for *chametz* in *ruchniyus*, too, although the physical checking is much easier."

He further added, "In the year 5525 (1765) the Ba'al HaTanya came home from Mezritch right before *Pesach*. On the day of *bedikas chametz* he would not eat, as he was completely occupied with his preparations for the *bedikah*, making sure to implement all the *kavanos* he had learned in Mezritch. That year, *bedikas chametz* took him the entire night, and he only owned one room!"

Contemporary Seforim

The Sdei Chemed once went to see the Toras Chedes. Knowing the *goan* was busy with his own studies and *chesed*, he commented that he, the Toras Chesed, certainly does not read his *seforim*, since it is a contemporary *sefer*. The *gaon* however surprised him, "I do look into your *seforim* and I have proof," and he started reciting the *sefer "Sedei Chemed"* verbatim.

How to Treat Seforim

Reb Shimon ben Tzemach, author of the *Tashbetz*, treated *seforim* with loving care. He even brushed the dust off them with a special silk cloth. In this merit, his reward was that the *seforim* which he authored would not ever be infested with bookworms. In all the libraries that the Rashab of Lubavitch visited, he noticed that even when the *seforim* standing immediately near the Tashbetz were affected with bookworms, that *sefer* alone stood untouched.

Seforim First Through the Door

The Maharil – a *Rishon* who is a major source for many current *minhagim* – would show his respect for *seforim* by telling anyone carrying a *sefer* to pass through a doorway ahead of him. This was to show respect to the holy books. Also, whenever a *sefer* fell, he made sure to personally lift it up and kiss it.

Returning the Books

Late at night, under cover of darkness, the *tzaddik* Reb Yechiel of Gostynin would sneak into the *beis medrash* of Kotzk unnoticed and return every *sefer* to its proper place.

The Balancing Scale

Upon recovering from an illness, Reb Elimelech of Lizhenzsk recounted what he had seen in the higher realms. "As I approached the entrance to the heavenly *yeshiva* of Reb Shmelke of Nikolsburg, I met Mordechai, the late book binder of our town. Knowing him to be a simple, unlearned individual, I questioned him how he had merited reaching such a lofty sphere.

He told me how, at his judgment, the *beis din shel ma'alah* brought all the torn pages that he had collected over the years from the damaged *seforim* and placed them on the scale. This had earned him a direct entrance into *Gan Eden*. However, since he was so lacking in learning, he first had to be taught *Torah*, beginning with *nigleh*, the revealed dimension of the *Torah*, and now he was ready to study *nistar*, the *Torah's* hidden dimension – at the *yeshiva* of Reb Shmelke."

Torah Lullabies

The Lubavitcher Rebbe regularly mentioned that mothers used to rock their small children to sleep with rhyming lullabies of *Yiddishe* content, such as "*Torah* is the best *sechorah* (merchandise)." The *rebbe* stated, "Some people think that it makes no difference what one sings to a young child, since anyway he does not understand. The truth is that everything that enters a child's ears affects his *neshamah* in the years ahead." A mother must therefore not only know about the importance of *Torah*. She should also sing about it to her child.

Lodging With an Old Friend

It is well-known, that the two holy brothers Reb Elimelech and Reb Zusha took upon themselves to go into a self-inflicted exile for a lengthy period of time. From village to village they wandered, dressed in simple rags, unknown to those around them. During their travels, whenever they would come to the town of Ludmir, they would stay by Reb Aharon, a noble but poor man. Many years later, after they had become famous, they traveled again to Ludmir. However, this time, they traveled by wagon with the accompaniment of an entourage of *chassidim*. As they reached the town, one of the wealthy townsmen traveled out to welcome them and invite them to stay in his luxurious home. The brothers however pushed him off, saying they already had their own accommodations.

As always, they went to the home of the poor Reb Aharon. The wealthy man came running and complained, "Why did you not accept my offer?" They clarified, "We are the same people who used to come here, and we do not want to change our place of stay. The only difference is that now we have come with a horse and buggy and therefore, you want us to stay with you. You know what, take the horse and buggy. Let them stay with you."

The Reappearing Dead Man

The story is recalled, in the name of Reb Yehoshua Rokeiach of Belz, that the Chida once requested a man from Chevron to accompany and serve him on one of his travels. During their journey, suddenly the man passed away. The Chida was quite upset, for now he would be returning to Chevron without the man. This would not appear well to his family and friends since he had left as a healthy, strong individual. Abruptly, as he was pondering this, the man reappeared and returned to doing his job just as before. He continued to accompany the Chida until they reached Chevron. There too, the man carried on as before, until the first Friday evening of their return. Then the Chida raised his hand heavenward, facing the servant, and called out, "*Dai! Dai! Dai!* (Enough! enough! enough!)" And the man simply vanished.

131

The Highest Point of Shabbos

The *Zohar* states that the highest point of *Shabbos* is during the late afternoon. *Raiva deraivin* – the time at which *Hashem*'s innermost will is revealed.

At that unique moment, after *Mincha*, *chassidim* continue to this day to gather to sing *niggunim* and hear *chassidus* in order to experience this *kedushah*. It thereby enables them to be inspired and empowered throughout the coming week.

Levushim

Reb Mordechai Yafeh, known as the Ba'al Halevushim or the Levush, was a *talmid* of the Maharshal and of the Ramah. At first, he had his own *yeshiva* in Prague, but after the *Yidden* were expelled from Bohemia, he moved to Italy. Some years later, he became a *rav* in Poland in several large cities. Towards the end of his days, he was the *rav* in Posen. He is most known for his *seforim* of *halachah*, however, he wrote many other *seforim*, all of which have titles beginning with the word *Levush*. He passed away on the 3rd of *Adar*, 1612 (שע״ב).

There is a story explaining how the *seforim* of the Levush received their unique titles. The Levush was a very handsome man. While he was in Italy, he became acquainted with a certain Italian nobleman, and would often visit him. One time, when he came to the nobleman's house to talk with him, he was away, but nevertheless, the nobleman's wife ushered him inside. She then locked the door behind them and demanded that he commit an *aveirah*. The Levush pardoned himself for a minute to use the bathroom, and from there he fled through the sewage canal. During the process, all the ten pieces of clothing he was wearing became totally soiled and ruined.

His actions caused a great commotion in *shamayim*. It was ruled that he would be given the merit of writing ten *seforim* which would illuminate the Jewish would forever. For this reason, he called his *seforim* "*Levushim*" – garments.

Taller for Shabbos

The Ba'al Shem Tov's tailor revealed that although the Ba'al Shem Tov's *Shabbos* clothes were significantly lengthier than his weekday clothes, on *Shabbos* this was not apparent, for they would fit him properly. Similarly, the *tzaddik*, Reb Chayim of Chernovitch, known as the Be'er Mayim Chayim, was a head taller on *Shabbos* than he was throughout the week. His usual place in *shul* was at the *mizrach*, near the *aron kodesh*, which was built with wings extending on either side. During the week, he would stand under one of the wings, but on *Shabbos* he could not fit under it and needed to stand nearby it instead.

The Clouds of Shabbos

The *melamed* seemed frustrated. He was attempting to teach his *talmid* the *gemara* about a person who forgot which day was *Shabbos*, and the child didn't seem to understand what he was referring to. So, the *melamed* explained, "Perhaps that person was traveling through a desert and forgot on which day he had left." The boy was still not convinced: "But how could a person forget?" The *melamed* challenged him, "In such a situation, how does one not forget which day is *Shabbos?*" The boy, who was to grow up to be the celebrated *tzaddik* Reb Yisroel of Ruzhin, clarified: "On *Shabbos* the sky looks completely different. You just have to look up at the sky and you will see when *Shabbos* comes in."

The Last Minute, Before Shabbos

Once, when the holy Ruzhiner was a small boy, he was playing in the yard on *erev Shabbos* before *Mincha*. His brother remarked, "*Shabbos* is coming," but he declared, "Not yet." To his brother's question.

"How do you know?" he remarked: "On *Shabbos* the sky is renewed, but I can still see the weekday sky."

After the passing of Reb Dov Ber of Lubavitch, the great *chassid*, Reb Aizik Homiler, was searching for a new *rebbe*. One *erev Shabbos*, when he traveled to visit the *tzaddik* Reb Yisroel of Ruzhin, he found him sitting and smoking his pipe, as was his custom. Suddenly, the last moment before *Shabbos*, the Ruzhiner threw down the pipe. At that very second, his appearance changed so much that Reb Aizik later remarked, "Had I not been there the entire time, I would have thought he was someone else. I saw that he ascended above while I remained below."

Moving Mountains

The Shach one time was walking on a mountain, deeply engrossed in thoughts of *Torah*. So much so that he did not realize he had reached the edge of a very steep cliff. Miraculously, at that instant, the mountain on the opposite side moved in, thereby saving him from certain death.

Place Your Trust in Hashem, Not Me

There was once a poor man who had to marry off his daughter. He decided to visit Reb Menachem Mendel of Kotzk and ask him for assistance. The *tzaddik* gave him a letter to deliver to Reb Moshe Chaim Rothenburg, a wealthy Jew, requesting monetary aid. Following the *rebbe's* instructions, the poor man trudged from town to town until he reached the home of Reb Moshe Chaim, where he was graciously welcomed. After taking a short rest to recover from his trip, the poor man handed the letter to his host and, to his amazement, he received a miserable sum. After all his *shleping* and traveling to reach here, especially with the letter he had brought from the *rebbe* himself, he was beside himself that this was all he was going to get! How would he ever cover the expenses for the *chassunah?* Having no choice, the poor Jew departed and began his long trek home. No sooner had he left than Reb Moshe Chaim rushed out to buy clothing, dishes, and whatever necessities a couple might need. He hurriedly loaded it onto a few wagons, took along an additional sum of money, and left to catch up to his visitor. Noticing his host with all his baggage, the poor man queried in wonder, "If you were planning to give all this to me, why did you have to put me through all that anguish?"

"Listen," Reb Moshe Chaim expounded. "When you arrived with a letter from the Kotzker Rebbe, you were sure you'd receive all you needed and forgot that we have an *Eibershter* on Whom we rely. I simply wanted to remind you to place your trust in Him."

Objective Advice

The holy Kotzker Rebbe was once probed how he gives people advice regarding matters of this world when he himself is totally divested and detached from all worldly matters? The *rebbe* explained himself: "I act objectively. Whenever there is a business deal, there always needs to be someone who is uninvolved in the deal and can give an objective opinion. So too, I, who have no dealings with the mundane world, am truly objective and able to give the proper advice."

Preordained Parnasah

A man protested to Reb Meir of Premishlan: "Someone is taking away my *parnasah*!" Reb Meir told him a *mashul*: "When a horse lowers its head to drink from a river, he stamps his hooves. Why? Seeing another horse reflected in the water, he becomes envious and angry, so he stamps at the other horse. He doesn't want it to drink up his water! You, however, surely understand that there is enough water for many horses. As our *chachamim* have told us, no individual ever takes away from the livelihood that has been preordained for another."

I Only Worry for One Minute

For the first ten years of his marriage, the *tzaddik* Reb Yitzchok Meir of Gur (better renowned as the Chiddushei Harim), was subsidized by his father-in-law, who desired him to be free to spend his entire day studying *Torah* and serving *Hashem*. Over time, his father-in-law lost all his money and the family was left poverty-stricken. However, Reb Yitzchok Meir continued studying *Torah* just as before.

One time, his wife questioned how he managed to sit undisturbed, free of any worry about their situation. Reb Yitzchok Meir explained, "Your father chose me for a son-in-law as an *ilui*, a person who can learn in one day what it takes others a year to learn. Likewise, regarding worrying. What takes others over three days to worry about, I can accomplish in one minute!"

The young *rebbetzin* asked further: "But what do you accomplish with your one minute of worrying?" He responded with a question: "And what does three days of worrying accomplish? There is no place for any of this, for everything *Hashem* does is for the best." A few days later, his brother Reb Moshe Chaim came to join him in his hometown of Warsaw. Having a good living, his brother purchased a home there and appointed Reb Yitzchok Meir as his financial secretary. And that was how Reb Yitzchok Meir supported his family, until one day he was appointed as a *rav* in Warsaw.

Increase for Us All

When the heads of the community got together and desired to give the Maharam Shik a raise in salary, he refused unless his conditions were met. He stipulated that he would only accept it if the *melamdim, shochtim, dayan,* and *shamash* of the community would be given a raise as well.

A Tetl Had Already Been Written

Reb Meir Yehoshua of Klimentov revealed that, the first time he was offered a position as a *rav*, he first made the journey to Rodoshidz to ask his *rebbe*, Reb Yissachar Dov, whether he should accept it or not. The *tzaddik* advised him to assume the position and proceeded to share the following story: "When I was a young man, I would spend months at a time visiting our *rebbeim* in Lublin and Pshischa and with the Maggid of Koznitz. Once upon my return trip home, while stopping in nearby town on the way, a *chassid* whom I recognized from my stay with the Chozeh, noticed me and was very pleased to see me again. He inquired about the state of my *parnasah*, and when I answered unenthusiastically, he suggested that I work as a *melamed* for his children. Recognizing the clear *hashgachah pratis* involved, I concluded that this must have been decided in *Shamayim*. So, I accepted the job without hesitation. I didn't even ask how much he would pay. After all, I thought, if it has been decreed from Heaven that I become a *melamed*, then surely it has also been decreed how much I would earn. I traveled to the *chassid's* home and began teaching his children. On no occasion did I ask for payment, and just accepted whatever money I was given. Having received it, I simply sent it off to my family to support them. At the end of the term I took my leave from the *chassid*, and according to his request, undertook to return after the *Yom Tov*, thinking again it was surely also determined from *Shamayim*. When I returned I fared the same way, accepting whatever money I was given without involving myself in the details of payments.

"Once the *chassid* questioned me as to why I did not make calculations and ask for my dues, as most people normally would. He said, perhaps I deserved more, and it had always surprised him that I didn't ask about it. I explained to him that he thought I was a tutor for him and that he oversaw my pay, but that was not really the case. It was all from *Shamayim*, I was working for *Hashem* and I trusted the Master of the world would provide the amount he felt I needed. After the second term, I took the final payment and returned to my hometown, Preshdborz. Not having a job now, I simply spent my days in the *beis medrash*, studying discreetly without anyone's knowledge. I became known as Berel *batlan*, a simple fellow who wasn't occupied with anything in particular.

One day, a Jew came to town collecting money so that he could marry off his daughter. Recognizing me from my days in Koznitz, he asked me to assist him in this *mitzvah*. I clarified that since I was regarded in town as a simpleton, I would not be able to collect more than two gold coins out of the total 400 that he needed. Therefore, I advised him to find someone more respected who could help him better. Nevertheless, he tried to convince me, suggesting that it was my *mitzvah*, since I knew him, but I maintained that I was unfit. As we parted ways, he muttered under his breath, 'I guess you were not on *Hashem's* *tzetl* (G-d's note).'

"After he departed, I attempted to understand what I had done wrong. What had caused him to say such negative words? This made me very disturbed. So, I hurried off on the road to find him and ask for an explanation. Having caught up with him, I asked how I had wronged him, he smiled and told me that he had not had any ill intentions. He explained that the Maggid of Koznitz had advised him to travel through cities and collect funds for a dowry. He told the *Maggid* that he found this very difficult, having no experience in fundraising. The *tzaddik* said that he should go to the first town to which he found a ride and added that a *tzetl* had already been written Above, listing those who would assist him to collect and how much he would earn from each city. He simply concluded that had my name appeared on the *tzetl*, I would not have refused his request. Hearing this, I reconsidered and decided to help him collect. After all, the amount had already been decided and it would therefore not depend on me anyways. It was market day, so I headed for the marketplace, stopped a merchant whom I had never met, and asked him for a donation. He immediately opened his wallet and handed me a note worth 100 coins! I realized that I had been put on the *tzetl* and continued to ask *Hashem* to help me succeed. With a light heart, I continued my mission and within a few hours managed to collect all the funds the *chassid* needed. I handed it to him, and then realized that the intention of the *Maggid* had been me."

Reb Yissachar Dov concluded: "Do not think that your acceptance as *rav* depends on the *ba'alei batim* or on the opinion of the community. You should lead them in a way that will bring honor to *Hashem*. Fear no one, and they will not be able to cause you any harm, for this position was given to you from *Shamayim*."

Don't Break the Keili

During the First World War, a *chassid* posed a question to the Rashab of Lubavitch if he should sell the forest he owned. He feared the German army was approaching, and the forest would likely be lost. The Rashab guided him not to sell and explained: "The Mezritcher Maggid said that if one has a functional *keili* for *Hashem's* *brachah*, he should not break it. Only if from *Shamayim* they cause it to break, then there is no other choice but to look elsewhere."

Being Wise Doesn't Mean You Have Bread

There was once a gentleman who was both a skilled craftsman and an accountant; however, he was unsuccessful in earning money. The Rebbe of Kotzk once drew him over to talk, "Do you understand the *posuk*, '*lo lachchomim lechem*.'" (simply meaning that a wise man does not necessarily have bread)? The man was silent, and the *rebbe* explained: "*Hashem* is telling a person, 'If you think you are a *chacham*, then go look for your *parnasah* yourself.'"

Just a Little Action Down Here on Earth

During one of his travels, the Ba'al Shem Tov went up to a home, knocked on the window and immediately continued his way. Upon hearing the knock, the homeowner rushed out and caught up to the Ba'al Shem Tov, wondering what he wanted. The Ba'al Shem Tov explained that he needed a certain sum of money, and the man fulfilled his request. However, the *talmidim* of the Ba'al Shem Tov were still curious about his actions. They asked him, "If there was a need to knock on the man's window because something was needed from him, then why did you leave right away without waiting for him to come out and hear your request?" The Ba'al Shem Tov answered that a man's request is fulfilled by *Hashem*, but He also wants that person to make some effort. Therefore, it was enough to do something small, like knocking on the window. Once he had done his part, he had no reason to stay and therefore continued on his way.

Crying for Pshat

The Mezritcher Maggid once called in Reb Mendel Horodoker, Reb Pinchas Ba'al Hahafla'ah, and the Alter Rebbe, in order to ask them a complicated question in *nigleh*. Afterwards, they departed from the *rebbe's* room to discuss the matter among themselves. Reb Zusha came over to them, inquiring what the question was that the *Maggid* had asked, but Reb Mendel Horodoker told him that this was not his domain. A few minutes later, when Reb Levi Yitzchak of Berditchev came in, the *chassidim* told him the question, and Reb Zusha listened in with a keen ear. Reb Zusha then went to another side of the room and began crying, "*Ribono Shel Olam*! Zusha does not have a part in the *Torah*, it does not belong to him."

A while later, Reb Zusha approached the Ba'al Hatanya, for he was ashamed to tell the entire group, and he elucidated a possible explanation. To his amazement, the Alter Rebbe declared that this was *Torah* from *shamayim*. The Ba'al Hatanya went right to the *Maggid* with the explanation, in the name of Reb Zusha, and the *Maggid* accepted it. This was always Reb Zusha's way, if he didn't know something in *Torah*, which was quite often as his mind wasn't as deep as that of his comrades, he would simply pray and cry with bitter tears. *Hashem* in His mercy would answer, and Reb Zusha was able to hold his own in *Torah*. For some scholars, the *Torah* comes a bit easier, while others must not only work hard but also must pray each time to understand the *pshat*. But either way, the *Talmud* says that if a scholar tells you that the *Torah* came to him easily, don't believe him. For the *Torah* is only acquired by one who is willing to give up his life for it.

Think Good and Things Will be Good

When the revered *mashpia*, Reb Michoel Beliner (better recognized as Reb Michoel der Alter), was still a young man, his son fell deathly sick. The doctors said that there was nothing they could do to help him. Reb Michoel went to the community *beis medrash* and shared his unpleasant news with the *chassidim* who were there at the time. Trying their best to encourage him, they assured him that *Hashem* would certainly have *rachmanus* and recommended him to travel right away to the *rebbe*, the Tzemach Tzedek of Lubavitch. Reb Michoel started to weep, saying that he would very much like to go, but the doctors said that it was only a matter of hours. If he took to the road now, it would probably be too late, and he would lose the last few hours he could spend with his son. One of the older *chassidim* berated him over this. He quoted from the *gemara* that one should never despair of *Hashem*'s mercy, and added that surely the good *malachim* would work to have the Heavenly verdict postponed until he reached the *rebbe*. One of those *chassidim*, a tailor, offered to join Reb Michoel on his trip, and together they set out. Upon arriving in Lubavitch, Reb Michoel was ushered in for *yechidus* right away. He later shared, "When I entered the *rebbe's* room and handed him the *pidyon nefesh* for my son, I thought to myself, 'Who knows what has meanwhile happened with him? The doctors said it's only a few hours...' and I began to weep. The *rebbe* read the note and said, 'Don't cry. You must have *bitachon* in *Hashem* with simple *emunah* that He will save your son. *Tracht gut vet zien gut*. (Think good and things will be good.) You will yet celebrate the *bar mitzvahs* of your grandsons!'" Not long after, the boy recovered completely. From that time on, whenever Reb Michoel had trouble he would recall the luminous face of the *rebbe* as he spoke those words, and the circumstances would change for the better.

When a person places his full trust in *Hashem*, feeling wholly at ease with complete *bitachon*, this is sufficient for him to merit *Hashem's* salvation. This is true even for a person who is seemingly undeserving, for the *avodah* of *bitachon* alone gives him the merit to be helped. This explained the deeper meaning behind the words of the Tzemach Tzedek, "*Tracht gut* – Think good and things will be good."

You Trust Hashem With Your Soul but Not Your Money

A simple Jew once paid a visit to Reb Mordechai, of Chernobyl, for *Shabbos*. When he requested a *brachah* before leaving, the *tzaddik* enquired about his daily routine. The *Yid* told him how he rose early, to buy merchandise from the local farmers, and returned home to *daven* upon finishing. The *rebbe* denounced this conduct, but the Jew excused himself by saying that if he *davened* first, he would be unable to buy the merchandise. Reb Mordechai then shared with him the following story: "A young man was supported by his father-in-law, but when his family grew he was forced to find additional means of support. He therefore left home and worked as a *melamed* for three years, saving every coin he earned. Eventually, having collected enough to start a business, he decided to make the long voyage home. On *erev shabbos* he reached a little village near his hometown, where he realized it would not be possible to reach home in time. He resolved to stay at a motel but was fearful to leave the money in his bag lest someone steal it. On the other hand, he had no idea if he could trust the innkeeper with it. Feeling that there was no other choice, he gave it to the innkeeper to hold for him.

"Throughout the entire *shabbos* he worried about his money. Immediately after *havdalah* he requested it back. Upon receiving his wallet, he counted all the gold coins and was happy to find that nothing was amiss. Then he continued to shake the coins and look through them. 'What are you looking for?' the innkeeper questioned. 'Is something missing?' The guest explained that he needed to make sure that his one copper coin was there as well." Reb Mordechai concluded his story, "Look at this silly fellow! After noticing that all his golden coins were returned to him, he still suspected his host of perhaps stealing one copper coin. You are doing the same thing. Each night you entrust *Hashem* with your *neshamah*, and upon awakening in the morning, He returns the gold you have given Him. So how is it you don't trust that He will give you your *parnasah* if you wait until after *davening?*"

And You Think You're Busy

Here is an excerpt from a letter of the Rambam, to his *talmid* Reb Shmuel Ibn Tibun, which describes his full daily schedule. It reveals the Rambam's absolute selflessness and tireless commitment: "I live in Fostat, and the Sultan lives in Cairo. The distance between us is 4000 cubits [a mile and a half]. My duties to the Sultan are very weighty. I must see him each morning to check on his health, and if one day he does not feel well, or one of the princes or women of his harem do not feel well, I am unable to leave Cairo that day.

"It often happens that there is an officer or two who requests my services, and I have to attend to healing them all day. Therefore, in general I am in Cairo early every day, and even if nothing unusual happens, by the time I come back to Fostat, half the day has disappeared. Under no conditions do I come earlier, and I am ravenously hungry by then.

"When I return home, my foyer is always full of people: Jews and non-Jews, prominent people and simple folk, judges and policemen, people who love me and people who hate me. A mixture of people, all of whom have been waiting for me to arrive home. I get off my donkey, clean my hands, and go out into the foyer to see them. I apologize and request that they be kind enough to give me a few minutes to eat. That is the only meal I consume during the day. After a few bites, I go out to heal them, write prescriptions and instructions for treating their problems.

"Patients arrive and depart until nightfall, and sometimes it is two hours into the night before they have all departed. I speak with them and prescribe remedies even while lying down on my back from exhaustion. Sometimes when night falls, I am so weak I cannot even talk anymore. Due to all of this, no Jew can come and learn with me wisdom or have a private audience with me simply because I have no time, excluding *Shabbos*. On *Shabbos* however, the entire congregation, or at least the majority of it, visits my house after *tefilla* in the morning, and I guide the members of the community as to what they should do during the entire week. We study together simple *Torah* subjects until the afternoon, and then they all return home. Several of them come back and I teach deeper concepts between the afternoon and evening *tefillos.* This is my daily schedule, and I've only told you a little of what you would see if you would come."

Pray Every Day for Food

The *talmidim* of Rabbi Shimon bar Yochai asked him a question: "When the Jews were in the *midbar*, why didn't *Hashem* make enough *mann* come down once a year to last for a full year?" Rabbi Shimon responded with a *mashul:* A king had an only son whom he provided with all his requirements once a year. However, he became dissatisfied with this arrangement, for the prince would only come for a visit once each year to receive his funds. The king changed the arrangement to give him his allowance day by day, so that he would be forced to visit more often. So too, a Jew living in the *midbar* who had several children would worry and say, "Perhaps the *mann* will discontinue coming tomorrow and we will all die of hunger!" He then had no choice but to trust fully that *Hashem* would provide him with all his needs.

Supporting the Tzaddik

Though the *tzaddik*, Reb Menachem Mendel of Kotzk, infrequently did not agree to accept money, at times he did accept support from one wealthy and scholarly *chassid.* However, one day this *chassid* became distressed to find that the *tzaddik* refused even his accustomed gift. Asking the *rebbe* for an explanation, he was told: "Every livelihood has a cause activated by *Hashem*, Whom sometimes removes the cause to test whether the person places his trust in the cause – or in *Hashem*, Who brings about the cause. If a man places his trust in the cause, thinking that his livelihood depends on it, then when the cause is removed his *parnasah* is cut off. If, however, he places his trust in *Hashem*, then another cause is provided, and his livelihood continues. In my situation," Reb Menachem Mendel explained, "your support has been the cause of my income. If *Hashem* should want to test me and remove my cause, you will become impoverished and thus be unable to support me. I would therefore prefer to remove the cause." The *chassid* contended that he nevertheless would like to continue, even if he became poor consequently. After declining his request many times, the *tzaddik* finally agreed to accept his gifts as he had done previously. Later that year, the *chassid* lost his prosperity and was forced to seek other employment to support his family.

I'm Praying Now, Everything Else Can Wait

Reb Shaul Ber Kobakov was a *chassid* and a successful lumber merchant from Minsk. One time while traveling on business, as he waited on the railway platform, he heard an announcement that his train would be delayed. With the extra time, he went to wash his hands and *daven Maariv*. Another Jewish merchant present, knowing that this *chassid* was not one to hurry through his *davening*, went over and cautioned him that his train would probably arrive before he completed *Shemoneh Esrei*. "That's of no interest to me," responded the *chassid*. "Now is the time for *Maariv*, so I'll *daven* now."

While he stood in a quiet corner and *davened* for nearly an hour, the train came and departed. When he finished, he waited for the next train and explained to the other merchant that nothing mattered to him, even his business, when it was time to *daven*. As he was speaking, just then the next train clattered to a halt. Before the *chassid* had a chance to climb on, whom did he see, disembarking from the train? It was none other than the owner of the forests to whom he was about to travel! That man came over and greeted him, explaining that he had waited for him at his station as planned. However, when the Jew had not shown up, he resolved to travel to him instead. From this Reb Shaul Ber understood that he must be anxious to sell his forests and was thus able to strike a good bargain.

Another time, this same Reb Shaul Ber went to *toivel* in the river before *davening*, with a few thousand rubles in his pocket. While immersed in his davening, he suddenly apprehended that his pocket was not as heavy as it had been before, yet he did not hurry to finish. He continued *davening* at his accustomed leisurely pace, and then put on his Rabbeinu Tam *tefillin*, and only when he was completely finished did he return to the river where he had *toiveled*. There, at the

place he had put his clothing down, he found his money –
completely covered. (He had most likely left it in the open and
uncovered). Was this done by the hand of Heaven?

If You Had More Bitachon

It had been an extraordinarily long journey, and the *tzaddik*
Reb Mendel of Bar, who was traveling together with the Ba'al Shem
Tov, felt thirsty. The Ba'al Shem Tov said to him, "If you will have
true *bitachon* in *Hashem*, you will definitely find water." After a while,
a *goy* approached them and questioned if they had seen horses
roaming around. He explained that he had lost his horses three days
earlier and was desperately looking for them. They replied in the
negative and then questioned if he had some water to share. "Sure, I
have!" the *goy* responded happily, and he gave Reb Mendel a drink.
Reb Mendel posed to the Ba'al Shem Tov, "If the purpose of the
goy's wanderings was just for my sake, to relieve me of my thirst, why
did he have to travel for three days?" The Ba'al Shem Tov retorted,
"Actually, *Hashem* prepared him earlier, in case you would exhibit
true *bitachon* because then your desire would have been granted
immediately!"

The Middah of Bitachon

Being faithful to the instructions he had received from
Shamayim, the Ba'al Shem Tov invited a group of his *talmidim* to
accompany him in a wagon to a certain town. The trip would teach
them all a lesson in the *midah* of *bitachon*. When the local innkeeper
saw them, he was pleased and welcomed them graciously. The next
day, while they were *davening*, a police officer sauntered in with a stick
in hand, banged the table three times, and left. The *talmidim*, baffled,
froze in their places. To their surprise, their host remained just as
cheerful as he had been before. A half an hour passed, and the same
officer returned, banged the table three times, and departed again.
Also, curious, the Ba'al Shem Tov asked the innkeeper to explain
these bizarre events. The innkeeper explained, "This is a warning.
He's reminding me to bring the rental payment to the *poritz*. It is
repeated three times, and if I don't bring the money at that point, my
family and I will be tossed into the dungeon." Hearing this, the Ba'al

Shem Tov remarked, "Judging from your calmness, you have the money ready, so why don't you go and simply pay your rent? We will watch your inn for you till you return, and then we will be able to take our places at your table peacefully." The innkeeper answered, "Truthfully, at the moment I haven't a single coin, but *Hashem* will surely not forsake me. He will provide the funds that are necessary. So, let us eat without haste, because there are still three hours left."

They ate together unhurriedly, and the innkeeper's face disclosed no sign of the gravity of his predicament. After the meal, the officer strode in for the third time and once again banged on the table, but the innkeeper, unruffled, remained calmly in his place. Subsequently he *benched* with *kavanah*, and the innkeeper went off to get dressed in his *Shabbos* finery. When he returned to them, he announced that he would now go pay and his dues. The Ba'al Shem Tov queried him again if he had the money he needed. Shaking his head, the host responded, "I haven't got a single penny yet, but I am sure *Hashem* will take care of me!" He took his leave and the Ba'al Shem Tov and his *talmidim* went out to the porch overlooking the road that stretched out before them, to escort him off as he set out on his mission by foot. From the distance, they all noticed a wagon approaching the innkeeper. It slowed down as he exchanged a few words with the wagon driver. The wagon then continued its way down the road. After a few minutes, its driver made a U-turn, called out to the innkeeper, and then handed him an envelope with some money. The wagon then resumed its route towards the inn, where the curious onlookers questioned the driver over the events that had transpired. "I had proposed a deal to the innkeeper," he told, "and offered to buy all the liquor he is due to make this winter, but he refused my price and continued on his way. Witnessing his stubbornness, but knowing his honesty, I decided to just give him the amount he requested for the goods. He then excused himself and rushed ahead, explaining that he was on his way to pay his rent." The Ba'al Shem Tov turned to his *talmidim* and said, "Look how powerful is the *middah* of *bitachon*."

Simple Faith, Parnasah to His Door

The *tzaddik*, Reb Noach of Lechovitch, told over the following story to his *chassidim*.

Hirshke, a simple Jew, made his *parnasah* by selling merchandise in the market. Each day before sunrise, he would go out to the countryside to meet the gentile farmers before they arrived in town, in order to bargain with them over their goods. Once a visiting *maggid* came to town and spoke of the intrinsic value of living with *bitachon* and explained that no man ever earns anything beyond what *Hashem* has ordained for him. Hirshke took those words to heart and thought to make a change. On the subsequent market day, he decided not to rush out early to reach the farmers before his competitors did, as was his previous way. His anxious wife, seeing him lying in bed late, urged him to get up. He explained to her what he had heard from the *maggid*, concluding that, whatever *Hashem* had planned for him, he would still be able to buy at home. She tried to use her persuasiveness to convince him otherwise, but Hirshke refused to budge. After some time, they heard the other buyers outside clinching their deals with the *goyim*. She pleaded with him again, but to no avail. Then one of the farmers exclaimed, "We're not selling any more stuff until Hirshke shows up!" The *goyim* began hitting the shutters of his house, shouting for him to get up and join them. Hirshke got dressed, invited the farmers inside his home and bought everything at a discounted rate, without even having to bargain as usual. From that day on he on no occasion needed to leave his house, for the *goyim* would come to him, and he made a respectable *parnasah* till the end of his days. Reb Noach ended the story and added, "This worked for him because he was a simple fellow whose faith was whole and uncomplicated. It wouldn't be the same for someone else who tried to upgrade his *bitachon*, by adding the sophistication of reason."

Kindness to All Creatures

Rabbi Yehuda Hanasi suffered for thirteen years from bodily ailments, due to the following story:

Once when he was teaching *Torah* in the *beis medrash*, a calf being brought to *shechitah* escaped its master and cuddled under *Rabbi's* cloak, begging to be spared. *Rabbi* rebuffed the calf, "Go! For this you were created." However, he should have showed more compassion, and for this reason, he suffered.

Thirteen years later, a maidservant was cleaning *Rabbi's* property when she found a nest of weasels. She was about to sweep them away, but *Rabbi* requested of her to leave them intact. Just as *Hashem* has compassion for all his creations so must we. After that, his ailments disappeared. (בבא מציעא פה ע"א)

The Taste of Shabbos

Rabbi Yehuda Hanasi maintained a good relationship with Antoninus, the Caesar of Rome. One time, *Rabbi* hosted Antoninus on *Shabbos* and served him cold foods, which Antoninus enjoyed as much as his hot catered meals from the palace. The Caesar came for a visit also once on a weekday, but this time he was served hot food. Antoninus noted that the food he had eaten the previous time had been tastier. *Rabbi* attributed this to a special spice that the food was missing, not wishing to explain more about *Yiddishkeit* than necessary. Antoninus remained curious what spice could be missing that couldn't be obtained this time. *Rabbi* explained, "The spice is the *kedusha* of *Shabbos*. I therefore can't supply this today. Do you have some '*Shabbos*' to supply?"

A Tzaddik's Fasting

Someone questioned R' Elimelech of Lizhenzsk, "*Chassidus* teaches us that fasting is not the practice in our weaker generation but did not the Ba'al Shem Tov himself fast prodigiously?" R' Elimelech replied: "After *Shabbos,* the Ba'al Shem Tov would go into the woods where he would meditate and pray in seclusion all week. He would take along six loaves of bread for the week. When he returned home on Friday, he found the sack to be heavy. Upon opening it, he was surprised to find the six loaves untouched. That kind of fasting is permissible."

Dancing Can Accomplish What Prayer Can't

One year at the conclusion of *Yom Kippur*, when it is a tradition to recite the prayer for the new moon, the sky was heavily overcast. The Ba'al Shem Tov became despondent that he could not have the opportunity to perform this *mitzvah*. He prayed zealously for the skies to clear, but to no avail. The *chassidim*, unaware of the master's despondency, began singing and dancing, joyously celebrating the forgiveness *Hashem* granted them on *Yom Kippur*. They danced into the Ba'al Shem Tov's study and requested the master to join them.

After some time passed, someone announced a break in the clouds and the moon was visible. The Ba'al Shem Tov said that, with their dancing, the *chassidim* had been able to achieve what his prayers had failed to accomplish.

I Stand on Your Shoulders

One time the Ba'al Shem Tov prayed the silent *Amidah* for an extended period which made several of the disciples become impatient. So, they left the room, and this caused the Ba'al Shem Tov to abruptly conclude his prayer. He then gently reprimanded them for abandoning him, saying, "If one wishes to reach a very high place, one may have to stand on the shoulders of someone who, in turn, is standing on another person's shoulders. If either of the bottom persons leave, the top person falls.

"As long as you were all with me, I could stand on your shoulders and reach the highest celestial spheres. When you left, I feel down."

Unconditional Ahavas Yisrael

A legend is told regarding the Ba'al Shem Tov's birth, which emphasizes the role of unconditional *ahavas Yisrael*. It is related that the Ba'al Shem Tov's father, R' Eliezer, had an open-door policy for all travelers and was hospitable to all. Once on *Shabbos* morning, a man carrying a knapsack and a walking stick knocked on the door and asked for something to eat. R' Eliezer did not reprimand him for violating the *Shabbos*, but instead welcomed him, serving him all the *Shabbos* delicacies. The man then revealed himself. "I am Elijah, and I came to test whether you would be hospitable even to a sinner. The reward for your unconditional kindness is that you will have a son whose *ahavas Yisrael* will be unconditional."

Gourmet Dishes in Beans

On one Friday evening the *chassidim* noticed a simple man praying with extraordinary joy and fervor. They inquired of the Ba'al Shem Tov, "What is it that gives him this intense exaltation?" The Ba'al Shem Tov suggested, "Let us follow him and see."

They followed the man to his humble hut and peered through the window as he greeted his wife with a hearty, "Good *Shabbos*," and joyfully sang the hymn greeting the angels that accompany a man home from *shul* Friday night. They saw that the table was covered with a coarse cloth, and except for two small candles, it was bare, without any delicacies.

The man requested, "My dear wife, please bring me the wine for *Kiddush*."

The wife brought two small loaves of challah, upon which he recited the *Kiddush*. He then took a bite of the challah and remarked, "What a delicious wine! Fit for a king! Kindly bring me the *Shabbos* fish."

The wife brought plates of cooked beans for both of them. The man ate the beans and stated," My dear wife! The fish this week is superb." He sang a *Shabbos* song and asked for the soup.

Again, the wife brought in another batch of beans, which he ate and then said, "What a delicious nectar!" When he requested the main course, the wife again served beans. "I have never tasted roast duck as delicious as this," he remarked.

The Ba'al Shem Tov turned to his disciples and said: "This man's joy in observing *Hashem*'s day of rest is so great that it enables him to taste the gourmet dishes in beans, just as our ancestors in the desert could taste any desired food in the *mann*."

So, my friends, next time you are served a tasteless meal, think for a second. Maybe it's not the cook but you who must have more faith.

Offer a Rebuke

Rabbi Levi Yitzhak of Berditchev sent for a wealthy man who lived in his town, who he knew could help him with an important financial matter. When he arrived, the *rabbi* implored him, "There is a poor man who needs assistance. I have asked all the others to give to a fund for him. But a substantial sum is still needed. I have no one else to ask but you."

"*Rabbi*, it pains me to refuse you. I obey every commandment, every *mitzvah*. You are aware of this. However, I will not give to any of these special causes. In fact, I wish you wouldn't trouble me in the future. That way, I won't be forced to dishonor you by turning you down."

Several months passed, and Rabbi Levi Yitzhak was visited by the brother of that wealthy man. The brother, Rabbi Levi Yitzhak learned, was destitute, had many children, and now required money for the marriage of one of his daughters. Naturally, he had already gone to ask his wealthy brother for assistance and was rejected. Rabbi Levi Yitzhak glanced at the man for a few minutes. Then he stated, "Do not worry. I believe I know what to do."

The following day, Rabbi Levi Yitzhak appeared at the rich brother's door. When the surprised man ushered the rabbi inside, Rabbi Levi Yitzhak walked to a chair and sat down. He said nothing.

Respectfully, the wealthy man stood opposite him, waiting for the rabbi to speak.

Rabbi Levi Yitzhak instead just smiled but did not say a word. After a long time, the wealthy man sat down as well. Even so, Rabbi Levi Yitzhak continued his silence.

An hour later Rabbi Levi Yitzhak, still smiling, arose and left.

The next day, Rabbi Levi Yitzhak arrived again at the wealthy man's house. Again, the wealthy man sat in stillness for an entire hour, waiting for the smiling *rabbi* to speak.

The third day, Rabbi Levi Yitzhak repeated the same actions. He sat quietly for another hour, and then got up to leave. As he rose, the wealthy man spoke up: "I can't bear this, *rabbi*. Why do you come here and say nothing? And why do you smile the entire time?"

Rabbi Levi Yitzhak settled back down into his chair. "Our sages say it is a *mitzvah*, a commandment, to give a rebuke when it will be heeded. And they also say we are commanded not to chastise when it will not have a positive effect.

"All these years, my friend, I have fulfilled the first of those commandments many times, but the second one? The people in this town have been eager to hear what I desire and to do what I ask of them. As a result, I have never had the opportunity to fulfill the commandment not to offer a rebuke. So, I smile in pleasure at fulfilling another commandment!"

The wealthy man turned red with embarrassment. At last he said, "What is it you wish me to do?" When Rabbi Levi Yitzhak voiced his request, he gave a considerable sum of money for his brother.

As Rabbi Levi Yitzhak departed the house, he smiled.

Ransom all Those Souls

Rebbe Levi Yitzchak, the Berditchever Rebbe, was a truly powerful personality. Under his leadership, the Jews of Berditchev were always imbued with eagerness to do *mitzvos*. For *brisim*, this was no different. They would arise very early wanting to perform the *mitzvah* even before *davening*. Yet, on one occasion, the *bris milah* of the *rebbe's* own grandson was delayed until late afternoon, and everyone wanted to know why?

The *beis midrash* was filled to capacity with *chassidim* pouring in from near and far, for soon the *rebbe's* new grandson would enter the covenant of our father Avraham. They waited patiently for the *rebbe* to arrive. As they waited, they sang a *niggun*. They studied, they recited *tehillim*, but the *rebbe* was yet to be found. Reb Yosef Bunim, the father of the newborn, was admittedly one of the more impatient folks. He walked toward the *rebbe's* private room and, upon reaching it, knocked loudly on the door, but there was no sound communicating from inside. The morning hours melded into early afternoon, and still the *rebbe* did not appear. Finally, the *shamash* decided to investigate the meaning of all this. He quietly walked to the door, bent over and peered through the keyhole. Walking away, he whispered, "The *rebbe* seems to be deep in thought. His face is fiery red, his eyes are staring into the distance, and he is breathing heavily. We will just have to wait."

Instead of the shuffling movement that permeated the room previously, the restlessness regressed into hushed silence. Nobody knew what was going on, but they thought it could be something serious.

A little past noon, the *rebbe* emerged from his quarters. The *chassidim* rushed to receive him, relieved that he appeared to be in good health. "Quick! Bring the newborn to me! It is time to perform the *mitzvah* of *bris milah*." The *rebbe* performed the *mitzvah*, and intoned:

"Our G-d…preserve this child for his father and mother, and may his name be called in Israel Moshe Yehudah Leib, the son of Yosef Bunim." It happened so quickly that the father realized his newborn son had been named without having been consulted. He was understandably disappointed. He had no idea of the name's origin; no one in his family or his wife's family had carried that name. Rebbe Levi Yitzchak whispered to him to calm him, "I know you have a lot of questions. I will explain everything. Very early this morning, I received a message that Rebbe Moshe Yehudah Leib of Sassov, of blessed memory, one of our contemporary leaders, had passed away. I sat down to contemplate this sad news. Then I had a vision that his soul was not directly on the way to the next world. I imagined that as his soul ascended, he stopped to gather souls that were in limbo, not completely righteous, and not completely wicked. The Heavenly Court watched and was confounded. Never had a worthy soul delayed entrance into *Gan Eden* because it was busy searching for those who were not completely righteous, not completely wicked. In my vision, I heard him talking to the Heavenly Court and demanding time to round up all the souls that were even partially worthy to ascend with him to *Gan Eden*. I sat here, as if in a trance, watching Rebbe Moshe Yehudah Leib Sassov ransom all those souls that he deemed worthy to ascend with him to Heaven. I knew that you and the entire community were waiting for me, but I was transfixed by the image. I could not move until the *tzaddik* had completely ascended to his deserved place in *Gan Eden*. And now you understand," the *rebbe* concluded his story, "why your newborn son was destined to bear the name of that holy *tzaddik*, may he be for a blessing."

Rabbanim For the Coming Generation

The holy Reb Meir Shapira would travel all over the world to raise money for the *yeshiva*. While trying to recruit the interest of one such sponsor, he said to him that his *yeshiva* would produce *rabbanim* for the coming generation. The listener challenged these strong remarks, "Do you think that all your 300 students will become *rabbanim*?!"

"No," Reb Meir Shapira responded, "three will become *rabbanim*. But the other 297 must attend *yeshiva* in order to appreciate the value and stature of the *rav!*"

Hashem is Everywhere

The Ba'al Shem Tov taught that working in a worldly occupation can be comparable to studying *Torah* and even greater. This is because everything in the world was created for the glory of *Hashem*. That is why, when a person uses worldly things in the way prescribed by the *Torah*, he is serving his Maker.

A man once appeared to tell the Ba'al Shem Tov that he had lost his oxen. He wanted to be told where they were. The *tzaddik* opened a *Zohar*, looked inside, and told him to go to the market city of Breslau. There he would find them. He later elucidated that *Chazal* say there is a "great light" hidden in the *Torah* that enables one to see from one end of the world to the other, and with that light, those who study *Torah* properly can see everything.

So, what is the moral of this story? There are those who separate the *Torah* from worldly matters, thinking that the *Zohar* is a holy part of *Torah*, while the ox is an ox, and Breslau is a market city! This is a mistake, for *Hashem* is everywhere, even in the lowliest things. Thus, the Ba'al Shem Tov also saw them, what could otherwise be considered mundane, inside the *Zohar*. This can also be seen from the special purpose that the oxen filled. They brought this *Yid* to the Ba'al Shem Tov.

Share a Torah Thought

Not all *chassidim* have the privilege to study *Torah* direct from a *sefer* all day. Reb Elye Abeler, a *chassid* of the Maharash of Lubavitch, was a businessman, and not particularly learned. Once the *rebbe* told him: "Elye, I envy you! You travel to fairs, meet many people, and during your business dealings you share a *Torah* thought and inspire the folk around you to study *Torah*. This creates joy above, and *Hashem* rewards such 'business deals' with the *brachos* of children, health and sustenance. The larger the fair, the more work there is, and the greater the *parnasah* earned."

Be Happy For Your Competitor

A shopkeeper one time complained to the *tzaddik* Reb Moshe of Kobrin that his neighbor, who sold similar goods, was much more successful than he. Reb Moshe agreed to promise him an increased income, on condition that he thank *Hashem* anytime he noticed his neighbor striking a successful deal. "It may be difficult to say this wholeheartedly, but after doing so again and again, you will find it easier." Reb Moshe reassured the storekeeper.

"As the *posuk* says, *b'ficha uvilvavcha la'asoso*: begin with your mouth, and that attitude will eventually permeate your heart."

Feeling Others' Pain

The Ba'al Shem Tov once told his *chassidim* of a case that was conducted in the Heavenly Court. The man being judged was a simple *Yid* who could *daven* and say *tehillim*. However, that was all he knew how to do. Yet, his *ahavas Yisrael* was exceptional. His thoughts, words and actions were all warmed by his feelings for other *Yidden*. He would personally feel their misfortunes and exulted in their joys. After considering his case, the *Beis Din shel maalah* declared that this unlettered *Yid* be granted a place in *Gan Eden* among the *tzaddikim* and *geonim*.

You Didn't Sigh

Once, when the Rashab of Lubavitch was just five years old, he and his brother Reb Zalman Aharon, who was over a year older, decided to play a game of "*chassid* and *rebbe*". The Razo would be play-acting as *rebbe* and the Rashab would be the *chassid* coming into *yechidus*. The Razo sat on a chair, straightened his hat, and the Rashab visited him for a *tikkun*. "For what are you asking a *tikkun*?" the Razo questioned. The Rashab replied, "This past *Shabbos* I ate some nuts, and later found out that the Alter Rebbe writes it is good to refrain from eating nuts on *Shabbos*." The Razo counseled him to make sure in future he would *daven* from a *siddur* and not by heart. "Your advice won't help, and you're not a *rebbe*!" exclaimed the Rashab. "When a *rebbe* answers, he is supposed to sigh. You didn't sigh, so your advice is no good!"

Bloody Soles

Once, during a freezing winter night, the Ruzhiner *tzaddik* stood outside to perform *kiddush levana*, his feet warmed with top quality fur boots. Some say the boots were even lined with gold. After a lengthy prayer, he turned to go inside, and the ground upon which he had stood had bloody footmarks. The fur boots had no soles. On the outside, the Ruzhiner appeared to folks as well-off and always refined, but it was only for *kavod haTorah*. Inside, the wealth meant nothing to him.

The Last Few Minutes Before Shabbos

After the holy Mitteler Rebbe of Lubavitch left the world, the esteemed *gaon* and *chassid* Reb Eizik Homiler, *rav* in Homel, was at a "crossroads" in his search for a new *rebbe*. On one of his searches, visiting the Rebbe of Ruzin, he watched as the *rebbe* sat smoking his pipe, as was his custom on *erev Shabbos*. Suddenly, an instant before *Shabbos* commenced, the Ruzhiner threw down the pipe, and his appearance changed significantly. This was so much so that Reb Eizik later remarked, "Had I not been there the entire time, I would have thought he was someone else. I saw that he ascended above while I remained below."

Inside I Loved Him

Reb Baruch of Mezhibuz sometimes would joke at the expense of Reb Levi Yitzchak. After-all he was one of the most unique characters in *chassidus*, always displaying his fervor for *Hashem* on his sleeve. Yet it didn't make sense, when one of his *chassidim* told him that Reb Levi Yitzchok had passed away, Reb Baruch became very bitter. He then locked himself in his room for three days, not allowing anyone to enter nor speak with him. At long last, Reb Hershele Ostropoler went in and asked, "I do not understand. During his lifetime, you used to mock the Berditchever Rav, so what is all the sorrow about?" Reb Baruch clarified: "When he was alive, I saw that *malachim* and *seraphim* were envious of his avodas *Hashem*. Therefore, I mocked him, so that he not be harmed. But inside, I loved him as my brother and respected him as a great *goan* in *Torah*. You know my brothers, so many times we see *machlokis* between *tzaddikim*. We get involved or judge when we should simply stay out of what we don't understand."

Not Feeling Honor or Pride

Once, when Reb Akiva Eiger came to the city of Poznan where he was to become *rav*, he arrived in a chariot, harnessed to strong stallions. With him sat his son-in-law, the Chasam Sofer, who had married his daughter a few years prior. The entire city came out to welcome them and stood cheering at the sides of the road. The Chasam Sofer, who understood that this entire honor was meant for his father-in-law on his appointment as *rav*, climbed off the chariot, and joined the crowds cheering at the roadside. But after a bit of time, he looked up at the other side of the wagon and to his astonishment saw his father-in-law, Reb Akiva Eiger, also walking at the side of the now empty wagon, apparently convinced that all this honor was being given to his illustrious son-in-law.

I Order You, Trees of the Forest

R' Yaakov Yisrael of Cherkassy was known to often give *kameyos*. Normally, *shalosh seudos* extended late into the night, however, one *Shabbos* the *rebbe* hurried through *shalosh seudos*. As soon as it was permissible to end *Shabbos*, he told his *gabbai* to take a swift horse and go to a particular village, to a certain person's house, and make sure he has his *kamayah*. When he arrived at the man's house, he found that he had already left. He was a dealer in lumber, and often traveled to the woods for more supplies. He had indeed forgotten the *kamayah* as the *rebbe* thought. The wife found it, and the *gabbai* took it and started out to locate him.

Upon entering the woods, he found that it was too late, a tree had already fallen upon the man. Curious, he opened the *kamay*ah, and it read:

"I order you, trees of the forest, not to kill this man.

157

Yaakov Yisroel B'harav (son of the *rabbi*)."

Extraordinary Vision

R' Yaakov Yisrael of Cherkassy used to put on his glasses by *hagba'ah*.

He explained his practice once: "I used to be able to see from one end of the world to the other. But this was interfering with my *avoda*, so I asked that it be taken away from me, except for once a week, *Shabbos Mincha* by *hagba'ah*, when I requested that the insight remain with me. So, I put on my glasses in order that I should see better during this time."

The Special Bed

As a young man, R' Yaakov Yisrael of Cherkassy was once staying at an inn. Not trying to draw too much attention to himself, he tried to appear like a simple man. However, when the innkeeper found out that his guest was a son of the Chernobyl Maggid, he had a gift for him. He said, "I have a special room for you." He unlocked a drawer and took out a little box which contained a key. He then led him to special quarters, a room at the inn that was usually locked. He showed him a high bed and told him, "You can rest here."

There appeared to be nothing special about the room or bed. It appeared slightly worn, from the many travelers that must have rested there, from their long journeys. "No sooner did I lie down on the bed," R' Yaakov Yisrael of Cherkassy recalled, "then I began trembling severely. Like the Patriarch Jacob, I felt, 'How awesome is this place. This is surely a G-dly place, and this is the gate to heaven' (Genesis 28:17).

"Straightaway, I went down to the innkeeper. 'What is the story of this bed?' I questioned him in all curiousness. He explained to me that the Ba'al Shem Tov had slept there during one of his travels. Upon hearing this, I went back up on the bed and had the most wonderful sleep of my life."

Chavrusas

The Alter Rebbe was the youngest disciple of the Maggid of Mezeritch and was especially dear to him. Evidence to this was the fact that he assigned his son, R' Avraham the *Malach* to learn both the revealed and esoteric *Torah* with him. The Alter Rebbe recalled, "We agreed that he would teach me *Kabbalah* for three hours. When the *Malach* was not looking, I set the clock back, and maximized my time with him."

Only the Positive Was Heard

The Alter Rebbe had the custom to be the *ba'al koreh* on *Shabbos*. After he left this world, the first time his son heard the reading of the *Tochachah*, citing all the horrible punishments that would befall Israel if it strayed from the *Torah*, he fainted. Upon being revived, he explained that he had never heard such terrible tidings before. "When my father read the *Tochachah*, one heard only blessings, not curses."

I Can't Annul the Good

While the Maggid of Mezerich was alive, there were no harsh anti-Semitic decrees, but these recurred upon his death. Some of his disciples became curious, "Since the *Talmud* says that *tzaddikim* are even greater after their death than in their lifetime (*Chullin* 7b), why does the *rebbe* not exercise his powers in Heaven to forestall these decrees?" The *Maggid* appeared to them in a dream and answered, "When I was alive and with my mortal vision perceived something as bad, I prayed to annul it. From my perspective, here I can see the good that will ultimately emerge from it. Therefore, I cannot intercede to annul a good."

Excusable Behavior

R' Dov Ber was privileged to married off his daughter to the son of R' Levi Yitzchok of Berditchev. During the wedding, R' Levi Yitzchok asked R' Dov Ber to deliver a *Torah* discourse, but R' Dov Ber refused. R' Levi Yitzchok then requested that the Alter Rebbe intervene. R' Dov Ber explained, "I cannot say *Torah* in the presence

159

of R' Levi Yitzchok, because he goes into so passionate a fervor that it will confuse my thoughts." R' Levi Yitzchok assured R' Dov Ber that he would not do so and would be on his best behavior.

No sooner did R' Dov Ber commence his *Torah* discourse than R' Levi Yitzchok began to gesticulate so violently that the table shook, spilling the wine and causing the goblets to break.

When R' Levi Yitzchok was reminded of his promise, he remarked, "What could I do? When R' Dov Ber began speaking words of *Torah*, the heavenly angels descended and began dancing joyfully to the sweetness of his words. Fearing the angels might be jealous (that a mortal has so superseded them), and try to harm him, I acted this way to frighten away the angels."

Never Be Oblivious to Someone's Cry

One time, the Mittler Rebbe was deep in thought, and he could not hear his infant crying. The Alter Rebbe, who lived in the apartment above him, came down and picked up the child to calm him. While this was happening the Mittler Rebbe was oblivious, and his father reprimanded him: "Meditation in *Torah* should never render you oblivious to someone's cry."

I Took it Upon Myself

While still a young man, the outstanding *Torah* scholar R' Baruch Fankel, known for his Talmudic commentaries and halachic response, *Baruch Taam*, chose R' Chaim (the future Sanzer Rebbe) as husband for his daughter, Rochel Feige. Shortly before the wedding, the young woman discovered that R' Chaim, her *chassan,* had a severe limp. She therefore refused the match. R' Chaim asked to have a few words with her in private, and she agreed to talk with him.

Although no one was privy to their full conversation, the story is told that R' Chaim asked his *kallah* to look into the mirror. He had something to show her that would explain everything. Upon looking at the mirror, she saw herself with a severe deformity. He then revealed to her that she, not he, had been the one destined to be deformed. However, since she was his *bashert*, he had intervened, sparing her the pain and discomfort. He instead took her deformity upon himself. That was why he walked around with a limp. Needless to say, Rochel Feige consented to marry him and they were both a light unto the world.

New Siblings

One time, the *tzaddik* of Sanz was given the honor of performing a marriage ceremony. As he was given the cup of wine, he closed his eyes and began meditating. Something seemed amiss to him. The family and guests waited impatiently for the *tzaddik* to begin the *brachos*. However, after a long pause, he abruptly set down the cup of wine and called the bride's parents aside.

"Did all of your children survive?" he questioned. The parents said that they had lost one infant, who was swept away when a river overflowed.

"Can you recall whether this child had any unusual birthmarks?" the *tzaddik* continued to ask.

The bride's mother affirmed, "Yes, he had a mole in the shape of an hourglass on his left shoulder."

The *tzaddik* thereupon had the bride's father take the groom aside, and examination revealed the mole on his left shoulder.

Then the *tzaddik* questioned the groom's parents, "Is this really your own child?" With a slight hesitation, they revealed that they had found him as an abandoned infant and had raised him as their own.

"The bride and groom are brother and sister," the *tzaddik* firmly declared. The joyous celebration continued, not as a wedding however, but as a reunion with a child they had thought to have died. Instead of *chassan* and *kallah*, the couple were now friends and siblings.

This incredible story of the *tzaddik's* prophetic powers spread rapidly through Galicia. The Tzaddik of Sanz tried to dismiss the happenings as nonsense. "I have no prophetic powers," he stated. "When I saw that I could not get the words of the *brachos* out of my mouth, I knew that something was wrong. I could not imagine what it was, except that for some reason, this marriage was not to take place. I could only guess what might be wrong and I just happened to presume correctly."

Have Someone Warm the Mikvah

R' Eliezer of Dzikov, who was a *mechuten* of the Tzaddik of Sanz, once became sick, and the *tzaddik* visited him. Upon entering the sick-room, he found the family beside his bed. However, R' Eliezer was sighing deeply and seemed pressured.

The *tzaddik* remarked, "*Mechuten*! What is all this sighing for? You know that it is no more than a transition as from one house to another or taking off one garment and putting on another."

R' Eliezer pointed to his family. "But I must provide for them," he explained.

The Tzaddik of Sanz reassured him, "No need to worry, *mechuten*. I will provide for them. I will be a father to them and care for them as for my own."

"But, Sanzer Rov," R' Eliezer remarked, "we are soon to have *Rosh Hashanah* and *Yom Kippur*. I serve as *chazan*, and you know that when I sing *ein kitzva lishnosecha* (there is no limit to Your years), the heavenly angels join in song and clap along with me. Who in the community can replace me for this important *avodah*?"

The Tzaddik of Sanz became very contemplative. "In that case," he requested, "have someone warm the *mikvah*."

The *tzaddik* remained in the *mikvah* for four hours. Upon emerging, he appeared exhausted but in good spirits. He said, "We can keep him with us."

R' Eliezer not only survived but lived for an additional thirteen years.

The Petition

One day, a Jew from Vienna came to Sanz. He appeared to know little about *Yiddishkeit* and spoke only German. He said that he was involved in a serious legal process, and although he was totally in the right, the judge did not behave kindly towards Jews. He was afraid that the judgment would go against him. The *Tzaddik* gave him his blessing that he should succeed.

The man appeared puzzled. "I was certain that the *rabiner* would draft a petition to the *Herr Gott*, on my behalf. I would like to review the petition to make sure that all the facts are correct."

The *Tzaddik* smiled. "No," he said, "the petition is very private. No one may see it."

The man was satisfied. It stood to reason that a petition to "the *Herr Gott*" must remain secret. "How much do I owe the *rabiner*?" he asked. The *Tzaddik* told him that there was no charge.

"But I do not wish to burden the *rabiner* without compensation," the man said. "It will certainly take much time to write the petition, and I must compensate the *rabiner* for his time and effort."

"Very well," the *Tzaddik* said. "When you receive a favorable judgement, you may send me three hundred gulden for *tzedakah*."

A brief time afterwards, the *Tzaddik* received a wire transmission of three hundred gulden with an expression of gratitude.

One of the *Tzaddik*'s faithful *chassidim* complained, "I have been pleading with the *rebbe* for several weeks for relief from my agonizing problem, with no result. Yet, this stranger from Vienna, who is far from *Yiddishkeit*, has his request fulfilled immediately. Why is he more deserving than me?"

The *Tzaddik* replied, "Do you think that wondrous acts are wrought simply? To alter any natural process, one places oneself, and all one's loved ones in jeopardy. This man was a non-believer, and to demonstrate to him that there is a *Hashem*, I was willing to make that sacrifice. Do I have to prove to you, too, that there is a G-d?"

He Immersed in the Mikvah but Didn't Come Out

While R' Yaakov Yisrael of Cherkassy was out of town, on an important venture, a man came pleading for the *rebbe's* help. He was the landlord of a small inn, in which he himself resided. The hotel was a frequent stop-off for poor wayfarers, for whom he provided food and a good night's rest. As a result, he had fallen behind in paying his rent. The *poritz* who owned the inn sent his hirelings to pressure his tenant to pay. He removed the windows, leaving his wife and children shivering in the frigid winter night.

Having no prospects of coming up with the necessary funds, to avoid the catastrophe, he went to visit R' Yaakov Yisrael of Cherkassy. When he couldn't be located, he told his tale to the *rebbetzin*. "The *poritz* has threatened to throw me into the dungeon if

I don't come up with the entire funds promptly." Her husband not being home, she recommended, "Go into the *beis medrash*, where you will find my grandson, Motele, studying. Ask him to help you."

The man did as he was instructed and poured out his misery to the youngster. R' Motele (later the *rebbe* of Hornsteipl) sighed. "If my *Zeide* were here, he would surely help you, but what can I do for you?"

"But the *rebbetzin* sent me to you. I know you can help me," the man wept uncontrollably.

When R' Motele shook his head sadly, the man arose and sternly said, "If you really are unable to help me, then I bear you no grudge. But if you can help me, but you refuse to do so, I will never forgive you, neither in this world nor the next world."

Upon hearing these strong comments, R' Motele turned pale. He told the man, "Get a lantern and follow me to the *mikvah*."

R' Motele immersed himself in the *mikvah* while the man stood above, watching and hoping for a miracle to occur. He didn't really have time to think that he was asking a young *bachur* to perform a *tikkun* that most adult rabbis are unable to perform. The pressure was just too much for him, he had broken. A few moments passed, and Reb Motele was still immersed. It was longer than a regular person could hold his breath under water, but R' Motele did not emerge. As he continued to remain under water, the man panicked and realized what he had done. He had endangered the life of this youngster. All hope seemed gone and now he had to rescue this boy from drowning. However, he couldn't move an inch. He felt paralyzed, as if bound by some unseen force. As time passed, he forgot his anguish. It seemed small, compared to the boy's life now at stake. He forgot about the *poritz* and thought only, "Please, *Hashem*, let the child come out alive!"

After what appeared to the man as a lifetime, R' Motele emerged from the *mikvah*. "You may go home," he said to the man. "The *poritz* will not harm you."

After a few weeks, the man returned to visit his *rebbe*, R' Yaakov Yisrael of Cherkassy, and told him about the incident. "When I returned home, the *poritz's* hirelings were restoring the windows. The *poritz* articulated to me, 'All night I could not sleep. I felt as though someone was choking me. I thought that perhaps this was because I had been so cruel to you and your family. It was only after I sent my men to restore the windows that the choking desisted. You can have all the time you need to pay the rent.'"

R' Yaakov Yisrael of Cherkassy sighed, "He is jeopardizing himself prematurely. The intensity of prayer to bring about such salvation requires a degree of *mesiras nefesh* that can endanger one's life."

I Know the Source of My Illness

Once, when R' Yaakov Yisrael of Cherkassy became seriously ill, the physicians did not know what to do to revive him. He slipped into a coma for several days, and R' Motele of Hornosteipel could not be persuaded to depart from the bedside. Finally, one morning, just as abruptly as he had fallen ill, he arose from the coma. He turned to R' Motele and said, "I know the source of my illness."

"The 365 *Torah* prohibitions and the 248 positive *mitzvos* correspond to the 365 tendons and the 248 organs in the body. The organs and the tendons receive their spiritual nutrients when one observes the *mitzvos* of the *Torah*. If I neglected any of the *mitzvos*, the corresponding physical part lacks its nutrition and is affected.

"During the days that I seemed to be unconscious, in fact I was soul-searching, and that is when I discovered the cause of my illness. It is my studies in the esoteric aspects of *Torah*. They caused me to become derelict in *Talmud* study. Understanding the source, I accepted upon myself to learn eighteen chapters of the *Mishnah* between *Minchah* and *Marriv* each day. As soon as I corrected my dereliction, resolving to improve my studies, I became well." And with that, he rose from his bed, completely healed.

Faith in His Rebbe

A Jewish grain merchant had a competitor who was not only an anti-Semite, but also hated him. Once, the two were together at an inn. The competitor had an assistant with him and, when no one was looking, he dropped poison into the attendant's drink. Suddenly the attendant began screaming with pain, shaking and fell to the ground. The anti-Semite told everyone that he saw the Jew place poison into the cup. "He was going to kill me, to eliminate me as a competitor," he alleged. The police were called, and the Jew, knowing that Czarist Russian justice wasn't fair for the Jews, ran for dear life.

Feeling desperate and having nowhere to turn, the Jew visited to R' Motele of Hornosteipel for advice. After a long wait to see the *rebbe*, he poured out his gloomy tale to R' Motele. The *rebbe* advised him, "Go buy a first-class ticket on the Parichad (the steamboat that traveled up and down the Dnieper River)."

The Jew was beside himself. Is he now going to simply return home as the *rebbe* instructed? He was confident he would be arrested and accused of murder! Nevertheless, his trust in the *rebbe* was still greater than his fears. So, he purchased a first-class ticket on the ship.

Full of anxiety and hopelessness, the Jew seated himself in the empty first-class cabin and began pouring out his broken heart to *Hashem*. He said *Tehillim*, sobbing uncontrollably. So engrossed was he in his prayers that he failed to notice the entry of two distinguished-looking individuals. One of them was a pathologist on his way to do an inquest on the death of the very attendant he was accused of killing. Curious as to why this Jew was so brokenhearted and weeping, they inquired what his trouble was. Feeling nothing to lose, the Jew told them everything that had happened. How he was set up, and that he was going to be punished for a crime committed by the other merchant who wanted to rid himself of any competition.

The two officials were impressed by the sincerity of the Jew's story. Upon arriving in town, they devised their own plan to come to the bottom of this narrative. They discreetly visited the merchant, inviting him to a tavern to hang out with them and talk. When the latter was inebriated, the pathologist began filling him with his own anti-Semitic tales, explaining to him all the troubles he had suffered at the hands of the Jews. The merchant was only too happy to share his own stories, finally revealing how he had rid himself of a pesky Jewish competitor.

As he entered the courtroom for the inquest, the Jew realized that the two people in the first-class cabin were the pathologist and the judge! The pathologist reported the merchant's confession, and the Jew was proven innocent.

My Divine Service Must Remain Private

Even as a youngster, it was quite evident that R' Motele had exceptional potential. He devoted all his energies to redeeming Jews who were imprisoned by the *poritzim*. On one of these ventures, he was exposed to the bitter cold for several hours. He developed a lung inflammation which turned into a chronic lung disease, which led to his premature death.

When R' Dovid found out about his son's illness, he visited him and requested, "If you accept upon yourself to assume a position as a *rebbe* and perpetuate our lineage, I will be able to secure additional years of life for you." R' Motele declined the offer. He desired his Divine service to remain private, and he would not sacrifice this to expose himself as a *rebbe*, even at the cost of his own life.

Service of the Heart

One time the great Talmudist, R' Chaim Elazar of Munkacz, witnessed R' Motele of Hornosteipel praying *Minchah*. He stood perfectly still through a long *Amidah* prayer. The Rabbi of Munkacz observed that his clothes were saturated with perspiration, as if he had been doing exhausting physical labor. However, he had simply been still in prayer.

The Rabbi of Munkacz told, "I always had difficulty understanding the Talmudic statement that the phrase *ulavdo bechol levavchem* (serve *Hashem* with all your heart) refers to *tefilla*, which is *avodah shebelev* (service of the heart). What kind of 'work' is prayer? However, upon seeing the *tefilla* of the Hornosteipel Rebbe, now I understand that silent prayer can be every bit as exhausting as physical exertion."

Feel the Pain, Then Return to Happiness

R' Motele of Hornosteipel's extensive library contained many treasured manuscripts, including a commentary on the *Talmud* tractate *Kesubos*, by R' Levi Yitzchok of Berditchev, and an only copy of his own *chiddushei Torah*. One day, a fire struck his home and the library was utterly destroyed. The *Torah* discussions of R' Yaakov Yisrael of Cherkassy were also lost as well as his own. His first reaction was a deep sigh. For a few moments his demeanor seemed sorrowful, but his cheerful expression promptly returned. He then said to his *chassidim*, "The *Talmud* says that one must express gratitude to *Hashem* when bad things happen, just as when good things happen (*Brachos* 54a). Suppose I had won the lottery. Wouldn't you have requested of me that I serve a *l'chayim*? If that is how we would have celebrated a happy occasion, we must do the same now."

In order to support their holy master, the *chassidim* asked for a *l'chayim*. One *Chassid* was bold enough to question, "But the *rebbe's* initial reaction was one of sorrow. Would the *rebbe* have been sorrowful had he won the sweepstakes?"

R' Motele smiled and said, "The *halachah* is that if one swallows the bitter herbs during the *Seder* without chewing them, one has not fulfilled the *mitzvah* of *marror*. One must actually feel and taste the bitterness. When *Hashem* causes something painful to happen, it has a Divine purpose. One should feel the pain and bitterness. However, he must realize that everything *Hashem* does is for the good. It is like a bitter medication, which is unpleasant but at the same time beneficial.

"My first reaction, therefore, was to feel the pain of the loss, but then to realize that, in ways beyond our understanding, it is really good."

Hashem Can Provide for One More

"One time," the Alter Rebbe said, "on the way to visit the Maggid of Mezeritch, I lodged at an inn in a small village. I questioned the innkeeper why he was living in a place where there was no Jewish community and *minyan* to pray in. He remarked, 'What can I do? I have my livelihood here.' I remarked in return, 'Do you think that *Hashem*, Who provides sustenance for all the Jews in a large community, will not be able to provide for one more?'

"Upon awakening the next morning," the Alter Rebbe continued, "I found that the innkeeper had packed all his belongings. 'I am moving into the town,' he said."

The Rebbe's Gabbai

A *chassid* once requested that R' Dovid of Tolna accept him as a *gabbai*. R' Dovid denied the request, explaining, "There are two types of people who do not have faith in the *rebbe*. Some because they do not know him, or his *gabbaim* who know him too intimately. Why should I take a *chassid* who does believe in me and make him into a *gabbai* who will not believe in me?"

Feeling No Pain

R' Motele of Hornosteipel once acquired a hiccough that persisted for many days. Despite all efforts at using various home remedies to suppress it, it remained. Because he also suffered from heart disease, there was concern that his heart might not handle the additional stress. Accompanied by his *gabbai*, they went to consult a neurologist in Kiev. The neurologist stated that the only way to halt the hiccough was by delivering a shock to the spinal cord. This was accomplished by heating an iron poker to glowing and running it down the spinal column. Since the time of modern medicine had not yet arrived, they agreed to the awful treatment. R' Motele said, "Nu," and proceeded to remove his shirt.

The doctor ran the red-hot poker down his spine, but there seemed to be no reaction from R' Motele. He turned up the heat on the poker. When R' Motele did not utter a sound, nor flinch even a muscle, the doctor was perplexed. He once again reheated the poker and did a second application, this time applying a lot more pressure. When there was again no feedback, the doctor threw down the poker and shouted, "I can't believe this. He is some kind of angel rather than a human being. Why, a short while back I had a burly Cossack here for this treatment, and I no sooner removed the poker from the fire than he jumped out the window. Here I have scaled him twice and he does not even react at all!"

R' Motele did not quite understand the Russian doctor's words so he requested his *gabbai* to translate the doctor's comment. The *gabbai* simply stated, "He said that the *rebbe* is an angel," and went on to tell about the Cossack who jumped out the window before he was even touched.

R' Motele smiled and explained, "Sometimes a person comes to me with his *tzaros*, and I desperately want to help him, but there is nothing I can do. If I don't jump out the window from my anguish at that point, I certainly don't have to now."

I Really Can Walk Again

Young and old, men and women, observant and secular, *Sephardim* and *Ashkenazim*, every type of person flooded the home of the holy *tzaddik* Baba Sali in Netivot, seeking his blessing and help. Everyone, without exception, held him in the highest esteem.

Once, Eliyahu, a man from Holon, was scheduled to have his legs amputated. His spinal cord had been injured by a bullet during the *Yom Kippur* War. He had already spent a lot of time in the hospital and had accepted his fate. The procedure was to take place the coming Friday.

The day before the surgery, a visitor who was an elderly woman suggested that he receive a blessing from Baba Sali before the operation. She told him that he had nothing to lose at this point by making the trip. She told how she knew of someone who had been paralyzed yet was healed through Baba Sali's blessing. Although Eli was not at all observant, he resolved to try it anyway, in desperation. "Maybe, maybe..." he thought, "You never know..."

It was not possible to receive permission to leave the hospital the day before the operation, so he had no choice but to sneak out. He told nobody, even his family was in the dark about his intentions that day.

So, he embarked on the journey to the *tzaddik*. When he arrived there, many people were waiting before him, so he sat on a chair in the waiting room like everyone else. After countless hours, finally his turn arrived. The custom was, before anything, to approach Baba Sali on his couch and kiss his hand, but because of the advanced thrombosis of his legs and the crippling pain that accompanied it, Eli was unable even to rise to enter the room.

Following Baba Sali's instruction, *Rabbanit* Simi, his wife, approached Eli and questioned him, "Do you put on *tefillin*? Do you keep *Shabbos*? Do you say blessings?"

"No," admitted Eli, and he burst into tears.

Baba Sali appeared to be moved by Eli's suffering and his sincerity. He told him, "If you do my will and observe the *Shabbos* and repent completely, then G-d, too, will listen to my will."

With sincerity and strong emotion, Eli promptly cried out, "I accept upon myself the obligation to observe the *Shabbos*, in all its details. I also promise to do full *teshuvah*, to 'return' in repentance all the way."

At Baba Sali's insistence, Eli was served a cup of tea. When he finished drinking it the *Rabbanit* suggested that, being that the *rav* had blessed him, he should attempt to get up, to go and kiss the *rav's* hand.

This was no simple task for Eli but with much effort and pain, Eli managed to rise. He couldn't believe it. His legs were actually obeying him! Shakily, he walked over to Baba Sali and kissed his hand! Joy and shock permeated him and the onlookers who saw this miracle. He began to thank Baba Sali profusely. The *rav* interrupted him, saying with a sweet smile, "Don't thank me. Just say: 'Blessed are those who sanctify His name publicly!'"

As if in a dream, Eli stumbled out the door and descended the stairs. He experimented, walking this way and that see if he was really walking. He had to know. Was he really awake? Could this truly be happening? With each step, his legs seemed to feel better and lighter.

Using his "new" legs, he walked over to *Yeshivas HaNegev*, not too far from the home of Baba Sali. When the *talmidim* realized they were seeing the results of a miracle that had just happened, they surrounded Eli, dancing around him. They sang words of praise and gratitude to G-d.

Celebrating in his new-found ability to walk, Eli returned to the home of Baba Sali in order to say goodbye properly and to thank him again. He also voiced his fear that his legs could relapse to their previous state. Baba Sali calmed him down, saying with pleasure, "Don't worry. In the merit of your oath to 'return' and repent, and especially that you promised to observe *Shabbos* according to its laws, which is equal to all the commandments, G-d has done this miracle and nullified the decree against you. Now it is up to you to fulfill your words."

As he was departing the home of Baba Sali's, Eli telephoned his mother. "I'm all better!" he called out, without explanation. Knowing his true state and situation, she assumed that fear of the surgery had caused him to lose touch with reality. "Are you coming home?" she queried with concern. "Or will you go straight to the hospital?"

Eli then explained to her what he had promised Baba Sali, the blessing that he had received from the *tzaddik*, and the miraculous improvement that had already occurred. As soon as he hung up, he then called his doctor at Ichilov Hospital in Tel Aviv, informing him of his cure. The doctor told Eli to return to the hospital at once, and to "stop acting crazy!"

Eli did indeed return to the hospital the following day, walking in like a normal person. The doctors could not comprehend what their eyes saw, that they knew was not possible. After several days and many tests, Eli was released without needing any treatment. Once again, he returned to Netivot to thank Baba Sali. The *rav* requested of his household that a *seudas hoda'ah*, a meal of thanksgiving to G-d in honor of the miracle, be prepared and served. Towards the end of the meal, Baba Sali blessed a bottle of water and told Eli to deliver it to the hospital so that his doctor could drink *l'chayim* from it. "And tell him," added Baba Sali, "not to be so hasty to cut off legs."

Baba Sali's *gabbai*, Rabbi Eliyahu Alfasi, [who witnessed much of the story and heard the rest of the details from Eli of Holon] stated that he once asked Baba Sali how he performed this great miracle. The *tzaddik* answered him innocently, "Believe me, Eliyahu, all I did was tell him 'Stand up!'"

Bless Me With Children

Rabbi Moshe Aharon Stern, of Jerusalem, told over a story about the holy Baba Sali. There was once a simple Israeli worker from Jerusalem, who had been married a long time but had never been blessed with children. The couple had visited all the specialists in this field of medicine, but to no avail. "Hair will grow on the palm of your hand before you see a child," the doctors informed him. Following many years of hope and despair, he had pretty much given up all hope of having a family. Then he heard about the great miracles wrought by the prayers of Rabbi Israel Abuchatzira, the great *tzaddik* known as the Baba Sali, of blessed memory.

With an expectant heart, the man journeyed many hours from Jerusalem to Netivot, to the home of the Baba Sali. Upon his arrival, he found a lengthy line of petitioners already ahead of him. Like the others, he waited his turn even though it took many hours before he could enter for his blessing. Finally, his turn arrived. He entered the *tzaddik's* room, feeling nervous, his eyes downcast, all the while clutching a small piece of paper on which he had written his only request: Children! He sat down and placed the paper on the table before the Baba Sali. The *tzaddik* looked at it, and then placed the note down. "*Matzav avud,*" was all he said. "A lost case!" Before there was time to respond, the man had been whisked out of the chamber by the attendants to make room for the next petitioner. Shocked, brokenhearted, he returned to his home feeling lost.

The following day, however, when the people started lining up for blessings, there he was again. As before, he waited several hours. Again, he entered, put his letter on the table, and yet again he heard the same terrible answer, "a lost case." Never giving up though, when the next day arrived, there he was again, and the next day again! If the Baba Sali was receiving people for blessings, the man would be there in line, at times waiting hours. Always he would hear the same miserable answer, "a lost case."

Finally, after almost a year, the family of the Baba Sali couldn't bear this any longer. They took pity on this man and approached the great saint with their own request. "*Rabbeinu* Israel," they pleaded, "this poor man has been coming to you for a year straight now, and every time you give him the same answer. Can't you at least tell him to stop coming already? It's much too heartbreaking to continue on like this."

"How long has it been?" Rabbi Abuchatzira asked. "We've counted. Today is his two hundredth visit." So, the holy Baba Sali agreed to talk with him.

That afternoon, the man entered the room in the same way as always and placed his slip of paper on the table before the Baba Sali. However, this time, the *tzaddik* did not even pick it up.

"Listen, my friend," he said softly. "You have been coming to me every day for a very long time now. Haven't I already explained to you that it is a lost case? Just go home, why do you insist on coming to me?"

The man lifted his eyes with a last breath of boldness. "I come to you every day, and I will keep coming to you every day, because I believe in the power of prayer, and I believe that G-d listens to your prayers, and that you are the only one in the world who can help me."

"Do you really believe that?" the Baba Sali said. "If so ..." he rose from his chair, "go out right now and buy a baby carriage!" (I.e. he blessed him in the merit of his great faith in *Torah* sages)

The man jumped out of his chair with joy and startled out of the room. "I got a blessing! I got a blessing!" he screamed feeling the bliss of the moment. He ran right to the children's store and purchased a beautiful stroller. That night he presented his wife with the beautiful new baby carriage. Nine months later, they had a child.

I Can See it From Here

A hungry visitor once came to talk with Baba Sali. As they were conversing, Baba Sali told his *shamash* to serve the fish in the refrigerator to this man. The *shamash* went to the kitchen and searched the refrigerator, but could not find any fish, and returned emptyhanded to Baba Sali saying, "There is no fish in the refrigerator."

Baba Sali responded, "check again." The *shamash* looked again but still could not find any fish and returned without it. Baba Sali insisted, "Please, there is. Check again." The *shamash* looked a final time, and found it wrapped in aluminum foil. Baba Sali turned to his friend and said jokingly, "I can see it from here, but he can't see it from there."

The Quiet of Shabbos

One frequent visitor to Baba Sali noticed that the bottle of wine blessed by Baba Sali, which was poured to hundreds of visitors, never seemed to become empty.

He also told that the Baba Sali did not speak on *Shabbos* (except for words of *mitzvah* such as *Torah*, prayer, *Shabbos* songs, etc.). The reason is that it says in the *Torah* that G-d "rested" on *Shabbos* from creating the world. What does it mean He rested? Did He have trucks and tractors? No, it means He rested from speaking. For this Baba Sali did not speak, in order to emulate *Hashem*, which is the purpose of life itself.

His Brachos Were Always Fulfilled

Baba Sali was once questioned, how is it that his blessings are always fulfilled? The *rav* gave two answers: First, it explains in the *Mishnah* in *Brachos* (ch.6) that one who drinks water out of thirst makes a blessing, "...everything came to exist by His word." Rabbi Tarfon says that he also recites the after blessing: "...Who created many lives."

"There is no water except *Torah!*" (Bava Kama 17A) When one who learns *Torah*, out of thirst, blesses, "...everything comes to exist by his word." Rabbi Tarfon implies that he can even revive the dead. This is the meaning of, "...Who created many lives." [Therefore, a scholar should be very careful reciting his blessings as they can nurture the entire world].

The second answer: *Samech, Ayin, Peh, Tzadi* (four consecutive letters in the Hebrew alphabet). The latter *Samech* is always closed. Why did the Holy One, blessed be He, make it closed? It comes after the letter *Ayin*, to hint to us that the *Ayin* (eye) needs to be closed and not see forbidden things.

Likewise, for the letter *Peh* which comes after *Ayin*. This comes to teach that the *Peh* (mouth) also needs to be closed and then a person becomes a *tzaddik*, which is the next letter. "And the *tzaddik* decrees and G-d fulfills." (Moed Katan 16b)

The Well of Water in the Desert

Once, two of Rabbi Yisrael Abuchatzira's daughters visited Paris, to participate in a family wedding. While staying there, they took a taxi to the city center to do some necessary errands. As they were riding, they happened to discuss family matters. The cab driver, overhearing their conversation, concluded that his two passengers were indeed daughters of the famous Baba Sali.

Upon reaching their destination and wishing to pay the cab fare, the driver refused to accept any money. The passengers glanced at him strangely. "Why won't you take our money?" they asked in disbelief.

"Because I always serve the members of Baba Sali's family for free. I would not dream of accepting anything from you."

"Why not? Do you have a personal reason for it?" they inquired.

"I know that your father is a holy man, for I have first-hand experience to prove it. Ever since a miracle happened to me in his presence, I have been his ardent admirer. I am prepared to serve him and his family at all times."

As they sat there parked at their destination, he insisted on telling them what had happened and why he was such a strong follower:

"Many years ago, when I lived in Morocco, I served as the chauffeur of the president of our community in northern Morocco. Your father, was the guest of our community and when he wished to return to Arpud, the president offered to send him home in his new car with me, a distance of seven hundred and fifty kilometers.

"I was well familiar with the long road. I knew that we would be crossing desert most of the way and would be on our own. I therefore equipped myself with all we might possibly need along the way.

"After traveling for a few hours, I discovered that the motor was overheated. We would have to stop and wait until it cooled off. I was surprised that a new motor should have become overheated so quickly and opened the hood of the car to inspect it.

"To my dismay, I discovered that all the water had evaporated. Without water in the cooler, to cool of the motor, we would not be able to continue. Yet here we were, amid a vast desert, stranded and helpless.

"I almost panicked, for the chances of finding water were nil and the chances of another car passing by, also close to zero. The prospect looked very bleak indeed.

"When your father saw my downcast expression, he stepped out of the car and asked what the matter was. I described our situation to him and urged him to get back into the car if he did not want to bake in the blazing sun. I climbed in myself, seeing that there was nothing to be done.

"The saintly Baba Sali sat down inside the car and sank in deep thought. A few moments later, he turned to me and said, 'Get out and start walking forward for about two hundred meters. There, on the right side of the road, you will find a spring of fresh water.'

'That cannot be,' I said. 'I know this area very well. I travel it frequently and I am certain that there is no well in the entire vicinity.'

"R' Yisrael insisted that I do what he advised. I dared not be disrespectful and decided to humor him. I started walking in the hot sun. After a few moments of walking I discovered, to my utter astonishment, a fresh spring of cool, clear water gushing by the side of the road.

"As you can imagine, I was overjoyed. I quenched my thirst and then filled a large container of water which I brought back with me to the car.

"R' Yisrael greeted me with a smile. He didn't say anything, but his eyes had an 'I-told-you-so' look. I poured some water for him. He recited the blessing over it movingly and drank his fill. I poured the water into the cooler and within a few moments, we were ready to continue our way.

"Before we began driving, however, I went to the spring and erected a sturdy signpost above it so that I would be able to find the spot in the future and so that others could enjoy it as well.

"The rest of the journey continued uneventfully, and we reached Arpud without mishap. I took my leave of R' Yisrael heartily and set out for the long return trip home.

"All along the way, I kept on thinking about the marvelous spring. When I neared the spot, I decided to stop and take a drink of its cool, refreshing water.

"I approached the place. It was distinguishable by the signpost I had erected there. I stopped the car, got out and approached it, full of excitement.

"I looked for the spring, but it was gone! I searched high and low for a long time, but it had vanished. There was no sign of it to be found anywhere!

"I returned to the car very disappointed. Throughout the long ride, I thought about the spring. I had plenty of time to digest the miracle that I had experienced firsthand. I realized that Baba Sali was so holy, the Al-mighty had created a spring of water in the midst of the desert especially for him, to save him from perishing.

"From that time on," concluded the taxi driver as he finished his tale, "I became an ardent admirer of Baba Sali. I consider it a great honor to be of some service to him or to anyone in his family."

He Had No Shoes

There was once a boy whose father passed away at an early age. His mother worked long, hard hours to pay for her son to continue to learn Torah in cheder.

Once, on her way home, the widow noticed her son sitting in the marketplace, shaking a metal cup, collecting *tzedakah*. "What are you doing here?" she asked in disbelief.

"My *rebbe* sent me to collect *tzedakah*," the boy answered in all innocence.

The widow was infuriated. She darted to the cheder for an explanation from her son's *rebbe*, "Why did you send my son to collect *tzedakah*?"

The *rebbe* saw that she was distraught, and asked her to sit down while he shared with her a story:

"One night, I had a dream," the *rebbe* related. "I saw my *rebbe* standing in the Next World. He was dressed in the finest garments, shining with light, but he had no shoes.

"I asked him, 'Rebbe! How come you have such beautiful garments — but no shoes?' And the *Rebbe* responded, 'I have such beautiful garments because I taught and learned *Torah* every minute. But I have no shoes because I didn't run to do chesed, to collect *tzedakah* for the poor.'"

The boy's *rebbe* turned to the widow. "I want your son to have golden shoes."

We Need Rain For the Mikvah

Nearby the dwelling of Rabbi Yisrael Abuchatzira we built a beautiful new *mikvah*, during the month of *Tamuz*, during the dry, sweltering summer. Having completed the structure, we lacked rain water, of course, to finish the *mikvah*. Our master, the Baba Sali, raised his eyes to Heaven, and proclaimed, "Master of the universe - You commanded us to behave in holiness and purity. So, we desire to fulfill Your will. Please, please, for the sake of Your great name, let it rain!"

Suddenly clouds gathered in the sky, and instantly, rain fell! In no time at all, the *mikvah* filled with water. However, there was a problem, we realized that the *mikvah* was not quite built according to the opinion of the Beis Yehuda, so we informed our master, our teacher, the Baba Sali. Straightaway, he ordered us to drain the *mikvah*. Someone spoke up in objection, "It does not rain like this in the middle of the summer," he insisted. "This is a rare miracle!" He then spoke directly to Baba *Sali*, and affirmed, "I take it upon myself, the sin that this *mikvah* is not perfect, built according to the opinion of the Beis Yehuda."

But our teacher, our master the Baba Sali, stood equally firm, insisting, "we are obligated to empty the *mikvah*." So we drained the *mikvah*, and fixed the design according to the Beis Yehuda, in splendor and perfection.

The Baba Sali then lifted his eyes to Heaven again for us and beseeched of *Hashem*. "Master of the universe, you know very well that we made this *mikvah* not for my honor, or the honor of my father, but rather, only to increase the purity among Israel, Your people. Please, don't turn Your face from us, and let it rain! Let the *mikvah* fill with fresh, new rain water..." Once again, as before, amid the dry, scalding summer, the sky darkened... clouds gathered... and rain began to fall.

Fire Stop Here

One time, during *Shabbos* evening, Rabbi Israel was studying the secrets of the Torah and probing the mysteries of the world. He became so absorbed by his study that he didn't notice that one of the *Shabbos* candles had fallen to the floor and began a fire. Noticing the danger, a family member promptly rushed towards Rabbi Israel to warn him. The entire house could easily catch fire.

Rabbi Israel simply took his cane and came close to the fire that was now beginning to spread. He waved his cane in the air and stated, "Master of the world! May the fire stop there!"

When the flames reached the spot designated by the *Tzaddik*, the fire suddenly went out by itself. He then returned to his studies.

Black Hands

Once, R' Motela of Hornsteipl washed his hands before bread and sat down to a meal. Abruptly, the *chassidim* sitting nearby noticed that their *rebbe*'s hands had turned completely black! The *rebbe* sat there silently for several minutes, until his normal color returned.

His *chassidim* pleaded with him to explain this extraordinary phenomenon, and he conceded by telling the following story:

"A certain *chassid* of mine, whom I'll call Yankel, once approached me and requested, 'Please, *rebbe*, you are the only one who can help me when I come to the Next World! After 120 years, I want you to defend me when my case is brought before the Heavenly Tribunal.'"

R' Motela answered that he would agree to assist Yankel in his request, as long as he would give him (so that he could help others with it) half of all he owned. "When the time comes," he said, "I will distribute your assets to worthy causes, and that will be a source of merit for you. In return, I will provide you with a letter for my father, R' Nachum, asking him to intervene on your behalf before the Heavenly Court."

Feeling satisfied with this arrangement, Yankel hastened home and divided all his possessions, returning with half the amount for R' Mottel. When he eventually passed away, he was buried along with this letter from R' Mottel.

R' Motela shared to his *chassidim* that unfortunately, Yankel's judgement was not in his favor, and he was not after all permitted to enter *Gan-Eden*. Feeling desperate, he remembered the letter from his *rebbe*, and informed an angel that he had a message for R' Nachum of Chernobyl. The angel responded that he could not permit him into the holiest chamber where the *tzaddikim* were. Nevertheless, soon the arrival of a great *tzaddik* would be announced, and then all the souls in *Gan Eden* would come out to welcome it. When that transpired, then Yankel would be able to see R' Nachum and show him the letter from his son.

It happened just as the angel had told him, and when he saw R' Nachum come forward, Yankel presented him with the letter from his son R' Mottel. To Yankel's astonishment, R' Nachum had long forgotten about this world. He told him, "The earthly world has no meaning to me. This is the world of truth and holiness." He didn't want to bring himself to read something from the world of confusion below.

Hearing his response, Yankel cried, "Is there then no justice in the world of truth? Where are half my riches, which I offered your son? He was my *rebbe* all his life and he gave me his word, here is the letter he gave me with his signature!"

R' Nachum meditated momentarily and was able to compose himself to read the letter. As he examined the letter, he was then able to focus better on the matter at hand. He instructed the angel to go to the Heavenly Court and state to them in his name that Yankel should be allowed into *Gan Eden*.

Explained R' Motela to his *chassidim*, "When Yankel began shouting that I took half his wealth and didn't keep my part of the deal, my hands turned black, because I had taken and didn't give back in return as promised. However, when he was allowed into *Gan Eden* my hands returned to their normal color."

You Didn't Greet Eliyahu

The *goan*, R' Zalman Margaliot from Brod, shared with R. Solomon Kluger that his uncle R' Sender of Satanow had taken an oath never to interrupt when studying *Torah*, for any reason. Once an old man whose face was awe-inspiring approached him, but the *goan* R' Sender would not interrupt his studies to greet him and welcome him. That evening he dreamt about his father of blessed memory. His father rebuked him and said what heroic efforts he had made to compel Eliyahu, of blessed memory, to visit him. When he did, you did not welcome him as befitted. Realizing what he had done and the missed opportunity, from then onwards, R' Sender's door was always open to every passer-by, and Eliyahu Hanavi came to him often.

He Would Toil and Toil

At first the holy Arizal, R' Isaac Luria, would toil greatly just to understand even one saying of the *Zohar*. Sometimes he would toil for an entire week. At times, he would be informed that this was the intended meaning of R' Shimon bar Yochai, but he still needed to understand it more deeply. Eventually, Eliyahu of blessed memory would come to him and he would attain understanding of both great and small matters, including all manner of wisdom.

I'd Build the Entire Structure All By Myself

While the *tzaddik*, R' Shalom of Belz, was occupied in building his synagogue, his older brother R' Aryeh Leib, who was at the time the Rabbi in Berditchev, came for a visit. R' Aryeh Leib had been an opponent to *Chassidic* philosophy his entire life. When he noticed his younger brother standing and working by himself among the bricks and mortar, the matter did not find favor in his eyes. He could not resist himself and felt the responsibility to rebuke him. "Our Sages say, 'When a man is appointed spiritual leader over the community, he is forbidden to do manual labor before three,' and why do you transgress the words of our Sages?" inquired R' Aryeh Leib.

"My dear brother," responded R' Shalom, "I must tell you that when I was still at Skol, I had three devoted friends with whom I used to study, and it was revealed to me from heaven: 'If a man does not slumber or sleep for a thousand consecutive nights, and occupies himself in the study of the *Torah*, then he will reach true spiritual perfection. We decided among us to remain awake and occupy ourselves with the *Torah*. However, not all of us made it through the count. One of my friends separated from us after a few hundred nights, and the second could not hold out after 800 nights, for his power of endurance failed and he could not stand anymore. So, I alone remained. On the final night of the thousand nights a mighty wind arose, such as can break mountains and split rocks. The wind shattered all the windows of the *beis medrash*. Even the candles blew out, and because of my great fear I wished to go home but the wind prevented me from going. Overcome by great sorrow and agony, I began to weep before *Hashem*. With great difficulties, I pushed my way through the strong breeze and I reached the Ark of the Law. I opened the Ark and cried out to *Hashem* out of the depths of my heart, until He had mercy upon me and the storm was silenced. At that moment, Eliyahu came and taught me the whole Torah. The last things he taught me were the rules for the building of a synagogue. How then can I award this holy work to another man? Believe me, my dear brother, if I only had the strength, I'd build the entire structure all by myself, from the foundation to the roof. However, the Holy One, blessed be He, knows that my strength fails me. But whatever I can do on my own, I do." Thus R' Shalom completed his words and the matter came to rest.

In the Name of Eliyahu Hanavi

"It was my custom, since I became *rabbi* of Ostraha, to close the gate of the synagogue each day following the morning prayer. The windows of the synagogue were tall and unreachable by the stature of a man. I used to stand alone in prayer, wrapped in my *tallis* and *tefillin*, continuing extra prayers. No one could enter the synagogue because the doors and windows were locked. I was accustomed to remaining there, until noon. When I returned home to eat, and afterwards, I would sit in judgement if anyone came before me. This was my daily routine.

"One day I was sitting in the synagogue meditating on the *Torah*, as usual, when I heard footsteps. I lifted my eyes and there appeared a man coming towards me. I was greatly terrified for I knew that the *shul* was locked and how had the man entered? The man observed me and saw how frightened I was, so he spoke to me with a gentle voice and said: 'I am a tailor from Lublin, flesh and blood like you are.' I questioned him, still a bit frightened: 'Why did you come to me?' He replied: 'Eliyahu, of blessed memory, sent me to you to warn you concerning the evil deeds of the people of the town. You must make good what is wrong for you are the *rabbi* of the place.'

"Then I questioned him: 'How did you enter the building? Surely everything is closed up.' Then he giggled and said, 'Why don't you ask me how I'll leave? Surely everything is closed, and the keys are in your hands?'

"I responded, 'If it is true that you are the messenger of Eliyahu Hanavi, why may I not see him? I shall not pay heed to all you have said to me until I see him with my own eyes.' He explained, 'I know your greatness and your saintliness, but in addition I know this, should you see Eliyahu face to face, fear and trembling will seize you.' I answered firmly. 'I wish to see the holy one of *Hashem* come what may. This for the sake of the honor of the *Torah* on which I meditate day and night.' The stranger then approached me and took a kerchief out of his pocket. He passed it over my eyes and my eyes were lit up. Then I saw Eliyahu Hanavi standing before me. Upon seeing him, I was so taken aback and terrified that I fainted, overcome by my fear. When the man revived me he said, 'Surely, I warned you that fear, and trembling, would seize you. Now it is your turn to make good on all that I have told you in the name of Eliyahu Hanavi.' He then walked in the other direction and left somehow. I checked all the doors and windows, and they were still locked tight. I have not seen him since that day. However, it was clear to me that this poor tailor was one of the thirty-six hidden *tzaddikim* by whose merit the world continues to exist."

Shas 101 Times

The Rogatchover knew all of *Talmud Bavli* and *Yerushalmi*, by heart. At his fingertips, he could recall the entire Rambam, *Shulchan Aruch*, and countless other *seforim*. Still he would constantly review *Shas*, making a *siyum* in honor of completing the entire *Talmud* regularly, every five months. One time, he requested that his family prepare a *seudas siyum* just a few weeks after a previous one had been held, on schedule. They questioned the *rav*, "Did you actually finish *shas* again in such a brief period?"

"Not exactly," he clarified. "This *siyum* is for a special *seder* that I maintain during unscheduled waiting periods. You know, people tell me to be ready for a *bris* at eight a.m., but they don't pick me up until eight-fifteen. Or they invite me to attend a wedding at six-thirty, and it does not start until seven. I have a special *seder* during those waiting periods, and I've just completed *Shas* in accordance with that *seder*." The *rav* indeed loved learning *Torah* and hence he had indeed completed *Shas* 101 times during his lifetime.

Surrounded by Seforim

The Imrei Emes used to collect rare *seforim* and manuscripts. Over the years, his library grew so vast that it housed over five thousand *seforim*, taking up 3 large rooms. He once confided to one of his close followers that he had learned through every single *sefer* in his library, otherwise, what was the point in having them? Whenever he purchased a new *sefer*, he would first learn it before placing it away on the shelf. Sometimes for days on end, he would remain in his library oblivious to everything else.

Once, the Sefas Emes noticed that his son was neglecting himself and depriving himself of sleep. He summoned his son and insisted on an explanation. "How is it possible to sleep when one is surrounded by so many *seforim*?" His son Reb Avraham Mordechai exclaimed.

The Spiritual Unity

The day prior to the new month of *Elul*, the Arizal sent the Meharchu, Rabbi Chaim Vital, to the burial cave of Abaye and Rava. There the Meharchu prayed fervently at the grave of Abaye. He thus merited through his prayers to unite the unities of the spiritual mouth and nose of *Atik*. While there, he was overcome with sleep. Upon awakening, he could not see anything. He returned to pray fervently again at the grave of Abaye and then achieved a great spiritual unity, mentioned in the book of the Gate of Holy spirit.

While at the grave of Abaye, he tried unsuccessfully to unite another great spiritual unity. A voice spoke out to tell the Meharchu, "Return! Return!" preventing him from achieving this great spiritual unity. The Meharchu became very afraid and shook with all his limbs from fear. His lips moved, repeating fragmented words, such as "What did you say? What did you say?" He could not restrain his mouth from mumbling. He wanted to ask about "the wisdom" to gain control, but his lips mumbled "the wisdom" more than twenty times without control. Then he repeated "the wisdom and knowledge" many times. Then through his lips came the words "The wisdom and knowledge are given to you," many times repeated. Then his lips spoke again, "The wisdom and knowledge are given to you like the knowledge of Rabbi Akiva."

Then he spoke, "And even greater than Rabbi Akiva." Then further came out of his mouth "like from Rabbi Yaba Saba." Then he spoke, "Greater than Rabbi Yaba Saba." The voice speaking from his own lips said, "Peace on to you." Then, afterward, "From heaven is sent to you, peace greetings." All this happened very fast and very wondrously. The Meharchu then fell upon his face in worship at the grave of Abaye.

After finishing, the Meharchu walked to the Arizal to ask him advice about what had just happened. He told the Meharchu that he had made the proper combinations of unities the first two times. The reason he was unable to make the third unity was because he had waited until the previous two unifications had been joined. When returning to the house of the Arizal, the Arizal saw with

Meharchu the soul of Ben Yehoyada, who was not from the source of Meharchu. The soul of Ben Yehoyada is revealed to all who reveal the unity revealed by the Meharchu at the grave of Abaye because it was the way of Ben Yehoyada in his life to reveal this unity.

The Arizal told the Meharchu, at the time of the afternoon prayer, that if on the next *Shabbos* he would merit to receive the soul of Rabbi Yaba Saba, this soul would remain with him like his other reincarnations. Through the presence of this soul, the Meharchu would ascend to even greater heights. Specifically, during the time of the *Amidah* prayer at the blessings of "the years," the blessing for "the springing forth of David your servant," and the blessing of "who hears our prayers." The reason for this is that Yaba Saba also is revealed to the righteous, like Ben Yehoyada. However, because Rabbi Yaba Saba is from the same source as the Meharchu, he would merit to even greater revelations through having this holy soul present with him.

On *Shabbos,* the soul of Rabbi Yaba Saba did indeed unite with the soul of the Meharchu. That Saturday night, *motzei Shabbos,* the Meharchu united in a Divine unity after midnight, upon awakening from his sleep. The soul of Rabbi Yaba Saba said to the Meharchu that, through this unity, he would comprehend all the wisdom he would desire. This unity he should unite three times daily. At the time of "the falling of the face" after the Morning Prayer, at the time of "the falling of the face" in the afternoon prayer service, and at the time of the recital of the *Shema* in the evening prayer service. When at midnight the following evening the Meharchu again had united this unity, the soul of Rabbi Yaba Saba questioned him why he neglected to make this unity three times daily, as he had advised. Through doing this unity these three times, the Meharchu would gain without end comprehension of the secrets of the *Torah.*

Rabbi Yaba insisted that he go to the Arizal to learn how to perform this unity three times daily. The Meharchu should ask the Arizal, who in turn would speak to the soul of Rabbi Yaba to gain this knowledge and then teach it to the Meharchu. Rabbi Yaba continued to tell the Meharchu how great his soul is before *Hashem,* as great as Rabbi Akiva and his associates. In the future, the Meharchu would merit to comprehend concepts that no other person had ever comprehended, even the Arizal. In the future, the Meharchu would speak with Eliyahu Hanavi, mouth to mouth. All this would come from making this unity three times daily. Great, and above all the men of his generation, would be the Meharchu. *Hashem* would give to him children and wealth so that he should be completely and independently wealthy. That morning, he visited the Arizal and told him of this conversation with Rabbi Yaba. The Arizal afterwards taught him how to make this unity during the three prayers. (*Shar Hagilgulim*)

Only From Hashem

Though living in abject poverty, Reb Shmuel of Karov, a *chassid* of the Chozeh of Lublin, decided that he would continue to ask nothing from the hand of man. Even if it would cost him his life, he would accept only whatever the Almighty roused the hearts of his brethren to give him of their own free will. He would not deviate from his principle for quite some time, even when the expensive holiday of *Pessach* approached. He was distressed, come *erev Yom Tov*, that he did not even have the wherewithal to buy a minimal *kazayis* of *matzah*, nor wine for the four cups, of *seder* night. However, he breathed no word to a soul, trusting instead that the Almighty would no doubt find a way to raise him out of his anguish.

Some miles away, a short time before *Pessach*, a wealthy *chassid* called Reb Shlomo of Kanskivli visited his *rebbe*, the Seer of Lublin, seeking advice. Upon his arrival, the *Chozeh* asked him to send Reb Shmuel whatever a family needs for *Pesach*. A simple task for the wealthy man! Late in the afternoon of *Pesach* eve, sure enough, an overloaded wagon trundled along the dusty track to Reb Shmuel's derelict cottage. It was highly packed with vessels and utensils of every kind. There was food, drinks and delicacies galore.

Reb Shmuel sat down at his *seder* table in the highest of spirits that *Pesach*.

Money, Pfui!

Reb Chanoch Henich of Alexander told how Reb Menachem Mendel of Kotsk once spent several months in Pshischah to study at the feet of Reb Simcha Bunem. He was so utterly penniless that he was clothed literally in tatters, but he was consistent in maintaining his principle of never requesting help from mortal man. Once, he was approached by Reb Feivl of Gritza who told him that Tama'l, the wealthy philanthropist from Warsaw, was soon to visit Pshischah that day. If he would simply call on her she would no doubt provide him with whatever he needed, for this was her custom.

The Kotzker heard and roared in disgust: "Money?! Pfui!"

Reb Feivl later testified that after hearing these two words from the mouth of the Kotsker, the desire for money aroused in him such violent disgust. It actually took several weeks for him to recover. For thereafter, as soon as he heard the subject mentioned, he would begin to vomit. Indeed, it took him some months of effort until he could even look at coins.

Honor Your Mother With Some Water

Reb Yitzchak of Vorki was always meticulous about showing respect to his mother. Every year he would journey to his birthplace, Zloshin, to fulfill this holy commandment of honoring one's parents. While there, he would sit at the Friday night table together with her, along with the many *chassidim* who accompanied him everywhere. They assembled in the house and crowded around the table to hear his teachings.

One time, his mother requested of her son a glass of water, but before he managed to move, one of his *chassidim* swiftly rose and fulfilled her request.

Leaving the glass on the table, she remarked to her son, "Yitzchok, it was you I asked, not someone else." The *tzaddik* rose promptly and ran to bring her another glass of water.

"The truth is that I don't really want to drink," she admitted. "I only wanted to give you the opportunity of being blessed with long life." This is the reward which the *Torah* promises those who observe this *mitzvah*.

Then she turned to the *chassidim* around her and said: "One isn't privileged to have a Yitzchak like this just from sitting and eating soup with noodles!" She prayed and worked very hard, as a mother, and servant of *Hashem*, in order to raise such a blessed child.

Supporting Torah Study

R' Chaim of Volozhin was the *rosh yeshiva* of the famous *yeshiva* in Volozhin, and he was also responsible for the institution's financial stability. It is a huge responsibility for a *rosh yeshiva*, not only to be responsible for the spiritual wellbeing of the students but also to daily worry about maintaining the place. Once, when times were difficult, R' Chaim traveled to one of the wealthy men who supported the *yeshiva*, to thank him for his pledges. While there, R' Chaim learned that the man had no family. He had one request of the *rosh yeshiva* that, when his time would come to leave this world, R' Chaim would undertake to say *Kaddish* and learn *mishnayos* in his memory. They both agreed, and additional money was sent regularly every month. The man became one of the main supporters of the Volozhiner *yeshiva*.

After many years went by, the man passed away from this world. It was a hot summer's day, but remembering his promise, R' Chaim traveled to the city where the funeral was taking place, and recited *Kaddish* there. After the funeral he returned home, went to the *beis medrash* and sat down to study *mishnayos*. During his studies, he encountered a very complicated passage which he could not decipher. Due to his exhaustion from the trip, coupled with the strain of struggling to fathom the *mishna*, and the extreme heat of the day, R' Chaim fell into a slumber.

The man who had just recently been buried appeared to him in a dream and told him, "*Rebbe*, I must thank you heartily for saying *Kaddish* for me. It was a major source of merit for my *neshamah*, as is your learning *mishnayos* for me. Regarding this *mishna* which you find difficult: I will explain it to you..."

Upon awakening, R' Chaim was astonished. He commented, "I recognize that if a person provides support for *Torah*, then in the Next World, he will acquire knowledge of *Torah*. I know that in Heaven he deserves to be granted *Torah* knowledge, which he enabled others to achieve during his lifetime on this earth. What I did not apprehend is that it happens so quickly! It is only shortly after his funeral and already he can explain a complicated *mishna* in *Seder Taharos* that I do not understand!"

Interrupting Someone's Torah Study

When R' Benzion Halberstam, the previous Bobover Rebbe, was refreshing at a mountain resort in Poland, he would go for walks accompanied by some of his *chassidim*. One time, he glanced towards the top of a hill, and swiftly dashed up the steep incline with his *chassidim* following. Upon reaching the crest they saw R' Chaim Sloveitchik of Brisk standing there, a *sefer* in hand. R' Chaim greeted the *rebbe* warmly, and they spent some time in his cottage discussing *Torah* thoughts.

Afterwards, the *chassidim* inquired of the *rebbe* why he had run up the hill. He explained, "As we were walking I noticed R' Chaim standing there, learning from his *sefer*. He happened to notice me and assumed that I was coming to visit him, so he ceased his studying to greet me. I hurried up as quickly as I could so that he should not waste another moment!"

Fear Hashem More Than Human Beings

When Rabbi Yochanan ben Zakai was on his sickbed, his *talmidim* paid him a visit. As was the custom when visiting your *rabbi*, they requested a blessing from him. He commented, "*Yehi ratzon* that the fear of *Hashem* will be upon you like the fear of a human being." The *talmidim* were surprised, "Is that all?"

He answered, "*Halevai!* If only that! For when a person is about to commit an *aveira* he makes sure that no one will spot him. If only he would fear *Hashem* the same way, he would be spared from many sins." (*Talmud Brachos* 28)

Honest to the Core

The *Tanna*, Rabbi Shimon ben Shetach, would sell flax for a living. He would carry his wares from place to place. Seeking to ease his work, his *talmidim* went off to the open market and bought him a donkey, from an Arab merchant. While leaving for their trek home, they noticed that he had accidentally left a valuable jewel hanging on the donkey's neck. Eagerly, they hurried to Rabbi Shimon and told him that *Hashem* had sent a *brachah*, and he would no longer have to toil for bread. Rabbi Shimon inquired, "Did the owner know about it?"

"No, of course he didn't," they replied. "If so," he told them, "you must return it immediately, for he sold you a donkey and not a jewel." When the *goy* received the gem, he exclaimed, "Blessed is the G-d of Rabbi Shimon ben Shetach!" (*Yerushalmi Baba Metzia* 82)

Too Much Gashmius

The *gemara* tells a tale about one of the greatest *chachamim*, Rabbi Elazar ben Arach. Once, he traveled to distant lands and partook of the pleasures there, drinking the wine and bathing in the springs. As a result, he forgot the *Torah* study that he had learned. Upon being called to the *Torah* on his return to the *beis medrash*, instead of reading, "*hachodesh hazeh lachem*" mistakenly he read, "*hachodesh hayah lachem.*"

The Maharash of Lubavitch explains the significance of these words, which literally mean, "Their heart grew deaf." They imply that the heart was stopped up. It became insensitive to *ruchniyus*, as a result of the pleasures of which he had partaken.

(שבת קמז ע'ב, סה"'מ תרכ"'ו ע' לא)

Don't Plan on Shabbos

During one *Shabbos*, while embarking on a walk, a certain righteous *Yid* noticed that the fence protecting his property had been broken. At that moment, he resolved to make the necessary repairs to secure his field's boundary. A moment later, realizing that he had planned mundane pursuits on *Shabbos*, he resolved that he would never repair that breach. He would leave his field open, unprotected. Because of his exceptional righteousness, *Hashem* caused a large fruit tree to grow in that exact place, which closed up the opening and providing him and his family with abundant *parnasah*. (*Talmud Shabbos 150*)

Simple Faith Provides

Chazal teach us that, although a person should have a trade, he must still *daven* to *Hashem*. This is because any trade can either succeed or not, and all depends on a person's merits. Rabbi Shimon ben Elazar stated, "Have you ever seen animals working for a living? Perhaps a deer working in an orchard, a lion as a porter, or a fox as a storekeeper? Despite their lack of work, they still have provisions, while I must labor for mine! It is only because I myself have caused this, through my *aveiros*." If a person would only have simple faith in *Hashem*, all his provisions would be easily given. (*Talmud Kiddushin* 82)

A Story to End This Book

"While he was in Dachau, a Jew who was being taken to his death, suddenly flung a small bag at my father, Judah Wallis. He caught it, thinking it might contain a piece of bread. Upon opening it, however, he was disturbed to discover a pair of *tefillin*. Judah was very frightened because he knew that were he to be caught carrying *tefillin*, he would be put to death instantly. So, he hid the *tefillin* under his shirt and headed for his bunkhouse. In the morning, just before roll call, while still in his bunkhouse, he put on the *tefillin*. Unexpectedly, a German officer appeared. He ordered him to remove the *tefillin*, noted the number on Judah's arm. In front of thousands of silent Jews, the officer called out Judah's number and he had no choice but to step forward. The German officer waved the *tefillin* in the air and said, 'Dog! I sentence you to death by public hanging for wearing these.' Judah was placed on a stool and a noose was placed around his neck. Before he was hanged, the officer said in a mocking tone, 'Dog, what is your last wish?'

'To wear my *tefillin* one last time,' Judah replied. The officer was dumbfounded. He handed Judah the *tefillin*. As Judah put them on, he recited the verse that is said while the *tefillin* are being wound around the fingers: *'Ve'eirastich li le'olam, ve'eirastich li b'tzedek uvemishpat, ub'chessed, uv'rachamim, ve'eirastich li b'emunah, v'yodaat es Hashem* – I will betroth you to me forever and I will betroth you to me with righteousness and with justice and with kindness and with mercy and I will betroth you to me with fidelity, and you shall know

G-d.' It is hard for us to picture this Jew with a noose around his neck, wearing *tefillin* on his head and arm, but that was the scene that the entire camp was forced to watch, as they awaited the impending hanging of the Jew who had dared to break the rule against wearing *tefillin*. Even women from the adjoining camp were lined up at the barbed wire fence that separated them from the men's camp, forced to watch this horrible sight. As Judah turned to watch the silent crowd, he saw tears in many people's eyes. Even at that moment, as he was about to be hanged, he was shocked. Jews were crying! How was it possible that they still had tears left to shed? And for a stranger? Where were those tears coming from? Impulsively, in Yiddish, he called out, '*Yidden*, I am the victor. Don't you understand, I am the winner!' The German officer understood the Yiddish and was infuriated. He said to Judah, 'You dog, you think you are the winner? Hanging is too good for you. You are going to get another kind of death.'

"Judah, my father, was taken from the stool and the noose was removed from his neck. He was forced into a squatting position and two huge rocks were placed under his arms. Then he was told that he would be receiving 25 lashes to his head, the head on which he had dared to position his *tefillin*. The officer told him that if he dropped even one of the rocks, he would be shot immediately. In fact, because this was such an extremely painful form of death, the officer advised him, 'Drop the rocks now. You will never survive the 25 lashes to the head. Nobody ever does.' Judah's response was, 'No, I won't give you the pleasure.' At the 25th lash, Judah lost consciousness and was left for dead. He was about to be dragged to a pile of corpses, after which he would have been burned in a ditch, when another Jew saw him, shoved him to the side, and covered his head with a rag so people didn't realize he was alive. Eventually, after he recovered consciousness fully, he crawled to the nearest bunkhouse that was on raised piles and hid under it until he was strong enough to come out under his own power. Two months later he was liberated. During the hanging and beating episode, a 17-year-old girl had been watching the events from the women's side of the fence. After liberation, she made her way to Judah. She walked over to him and said, 'I've lost everyone. I don't want to be alone any more. I saw what you did that day when the officer wanted to hang you. Will you marry me?' My parents walked over to the Klausenberger Rebbe and requested that he perform the marriage ceremony. The Klausenberger Rebbe, whose *Kiddush Hashem* is legendary, wrote out a *kesubah* [marriage contract] by hand from memory and married the couple. I have that handwritten *kesubah* in my possession to this day." (Rabbi Yosef Wallis Via Max E)

Glossary

Abba- Father
Achdus- Togetherness
Ahavas Yisrael- Love of one's fellow Jew
Al naharos Bavel- Prayer said about the Destruction of the Temple
Aliyah to the Holy Land- Emigrating to Israel
Am Haaretz- Common Jewish Man, sometimes referring to someone unlearned in Jewish laws
Am Yisrael- Jewish Nation
Amen- Used after a prayer, or other formal statement to express solemn ratification or agreement
Amidah- See definition of *Shmoneh Esrey*
Amorah- Their legal discussions and debates were eventually codified in the *Gemara*. The *Amoraim* followed the *Tannaim* in the sequence of ancient Jewish scholars.
Aron Hakodesh- The Torah ark or ark in a synagogue
Aseres Hadibros- The Ten Commandments
Atik- Ancient
Av Beis Din- The head of the Jewish court
Aveirah / Aveiros- Sin / Sins
Avenu- Our father
Avodah- Service
Avodas Hashem- Service to G-d
Avos- Forefathers
Avrechim- Married men who learn in Kollel
Ba'al koreh- The individual who chants Torah from the scroll at the synagogue
Ba'alei Batim- Working men
Bar-mitzvah- A ceremony and celebration for a Jewish boy at the age of 13 when he takes on the religious duties and responsibilities
Baruch Hashem- Blessed is Hashem
Bashert- Soulmate or destined
Batlan- An unemployed Jewish man who spends most of his time in the synagogue or study hall or who is available for making up the number required for religious services or for singing prayers in the memory of the dead
Bedikas chametz- Checking for unleavened bread before Passover
Beis Din- Jewish Court
Beis Din Shel Maalah- Court in Heaven
Beis Hamedrash / Beis Medrash- House of Study, Synagogue
Beis Hamikdash- The Jewish Temple in Jerusalem
Bekishe- Decorative coat worn on Shabbos by chassidish men

Ben- Son
Benched- Blessed
B'gashmius- In physical matters
Birkas hamazon- Blessings after eating bread
Bitachon- Faith
Bittul- Nulify
Blatt- Pages of Talmud
Bnei Yisroel- Children of Israel
Bochor / Bochorim- Young Single Man/men
Borchu- Blessing said during the Marriv prayer recited by the Chazan
Boruch Hashem- Thank Hashem
Brachah- Blessing
Brachah Shehakol- Blessing over eating food
Bris Milah / Brisim- Circumcision
B'ruchnius- Spiritual benefits
Chacham- Wise man
Chaim- Life
Chalav Yisrael- Cow milked by a Jew
Chalukah- Traditionally the first hair-cut of a boy at age 3
Chas v'shalom- It shouldn't happen
Chassan- Bridegroom
Chassid- Follower or person seeking higher purity
Chassunah- Wedding
Chatzos- Midday or Midnight
Chavrusah- Study partner
Chazal- Sages
Chazan- Prayer leader in the synagogue
Cheder- Religious school for boys
Chevrah Kaddisha- The local burial society
Chiddushei Torah- Original *Torah* insights
Chachmah- Wisdom
Cholent- Hot meat dish traditionally served for *Shabbos* Lunch
Chovos Halevavos- A Main work in Jewish literature, Duties of the Heart by Rabeinu Bachya ibn Paquda zt'l
Chozen- Breastplate worn by the *Kohen hagadol*
Chumash- Five books of Moses
Churban- Destruction (of the Temple)
Daven / Davened- Pray, Prayed
Dayan- Judge
Der heiliker- The Holy Man
Divrei Torah- Words of Torah
Drush- Homiletic interpretation of the Torah
D'veikus- Closeness to G-d
Eibeshter- G-d in Yiddish
Ein K'Elokeinu- There is None like Our G-d
Eliyahu Hanavi- Elijah the Prophet
Emunah- Faith
Eretz Hakodesh- The holy land
Eretz Yisrael- Holy Land (of Israel)

Erev- Evening before

Farbrengen- Feast made by *Chassidim*

Gabbai- Aramaic) (a) the person responsible for the proper functioning of a synagogue or communal body (b) an official of the Rebbe's court, who admits people for yechidus, private meetings

Galil- Northern Israel

Gan Eden- Garden of Eden

Gaon- Great rabbinical scholar

Gemara- Talmud

Gematria- Numerical value of the Hebrew letters

Gemilus Chassadim- Kindness to others

Geonim- Great Sages

Gilgul- Reincarnation

Goy / Goyim / Goyishe- Non-Jew(s), literally means nations

Gut- Good in Yiddish

Hagadah- Book recited at the *Seder* on Passover

Hagba'ah- The ceremony of lifting the Torah

Halachah- Jewish Law

Halevai- Arameic for "if only"

Har Sinai- Mountain where the Jews received the Torah

Hareini mekabel- I accept upon myself

Hashem- G-d

Hashgacha Pratis- Everything comes from *Hashem*; personal supervision

Haskamah- Approbation

Havdalah- Prayer to conclude the *Shabbos*

Heichalos- The heavenly mansion

Hiddur Mitzvah- "The beautification of a *mitzvah*," actions that glorify, or beautify, the observances and celebrations within Jewish tradition

Hillulah- Memorial

Im Yirtze Hashem- With the help of G-d

Kaddish- Recited for the deceased soul

Kadoshim- Holy Sacrifice

Kallah- Bride

Kameyos- Amulets

Kaparah- Forgiveness

Kavanah- Concentration, intent. The frame of mind required for prayer or performance of a mitzvah (commandment)

Kavod Hatorah- Respect for the Torah or Sage

Kazayis- Talmudic unit of volume approximately equal to the size of an average olive.

Kedushah- Holiness

Keili- Vessel

Kerias hatorah- Reciting the Torah in a Minyan of 10 Men

Kever- Grave

Kiddush- Blessing recited on *Shabbos* over a cup of wine

Kiddush Levana- Blessing over the new moon recited monthly

Klal Yisrael- Jewish nation

Kohen- Jewish priests

Kohanim- Jewish priests

Kohen Gadol- Head Jewish priest

Korbanos- Sacrifices

Kriyas Shemah- Recital of the Shema

Ksav yad- Personal handwriting

Lag b'Omer- A Jewish holiday, celebrated on the 33rd day of the counting of the Omer, commemorating the end of Rabbi Akiva's students dying. It is also the memorial of Rebbe Shimon Bar Yochai.

L'Chayim- a word used to express good wishes just before drinking an alcoholic drink

L'chovod Shabbos Kodesh- In honor of the holy *Shabbos*

Le'illui Nishmas- For the sake of the deceased

Levi- 1) A descendant of the tribe of Levi, which was set aside to perform certain duties in connection with the Temple; 2) Son of Jacob (Israel). Ancestor of the tribe of Levi.

Levushim- Clothes

Lishmah- With pure intentions

L'shem Shamayim- For the sake of *Hashem* alone

Ma'ariv- West, also evening service

Ma'aseh Merkavah- Works of the Chariot

Machlokes- Controversy

Madrega- Level where a person is holding in spirituality

Maggid- Story teller, sometimes referring to R. Dov Ber Mezritch, Leader of *Chassidus* after the Baal Shem Tov

Malach / Malochim- Angel(s)

Mamash- Really

Mann- The food that fell from the sky to feed the wandering Israelites in the Bible

Marror- Bitter herb used on Passover

Mashpiah- Spiritual guide

Mashul- Comparison or parable

Matzah- Unleavened bread

Mechuten- Father-in-law

Melamdim / Melamed- Teachers/teacher

Mesiras Nefesh- Self-sacrifice

Mezuzah- A scroll placed on doorposts of Jewish homes, containing a section from the Torah and often enclosed in a decorative case

Midbar- Desert

Middos- Character Traits

Mikveh- Ritual Bath house

Minchah- Afternoon prayer service

Minhag- Tradition or custom

Minyan- Quorum of 10 men during the prayer service

Mishnah / Mishnayos- The first compilation of the oral law, authored by Rabbi Yehudah HaNasi; the germinal statements of law elucidated by the *Gemara*

Misnagedim- Opposers

Mitzvos- Commandments

Mizbeiach- The Altar in the Temple

Mizrach- East

Moshe Rabbeinu- Moses, Greatest prophet who ever lived.

Moshiach- The anointed one, who will herald in a new era for Judaism and all humankind.

Motzei- The leaving of, often used to mean the night after

Mussar- The study of character correction

Nachas- Pride or gratification, especially at the achievements of one's children

Nagid- Prince or leader

Neshamah- Soul

Niggun / Niggunim- Melody(s)

Nigleh- The revealed aspects of the Torah

Nishmas/ Nishmas Kol Chai- The breath of every living thing) is a Jewish prayer that is recited following the Song of the Sea

Nistar- Hidden

Olam Habah- The World to Come

Parnasah- Income

Parsha- Weekly portion read from the *Torah* on *Shabbos*

Parshios- Parchments

Pasuk- Verse

Pasul- Unfit

Perush- Commentary

Peyos- Sidelocks

Pesach- Passover holiday

Pidyon / Pidyon nefesh- Redemption for the soul, in form of a note and money given to a sage

Pilpul- Loosely meaning "sharp analysis"; refers to a method of studying the *Talmud* through intense textual analysis in attempts to either explain conceptual differences between various halakhic rulings or to reconcile any apparent contradictions presented from various readings of different texts.

Poritz- Nobelman

Posuk / Posukim- Verse, Verses

Pshat- Simplest meaning, based on the text and context

Rabbanim- Sages

Rabbanit- See **Rebbetzyn**

Rabbi- Jewish scholar or teacher

Rachmonus- Mercy

Raphael- The angel of healing

Rav- Rabbi who answers halacha questions

Rebbe- A rabbi, or rabbinic leader of a Chassidic sect

Rebbetzyn- The Rabbi's Wife

Remez- Meaning "hint" in reference to scriptural interpretations

Ribono Shel Olam- Master of the World

Rishon- First

Rishonim- The leading *rabbis* and poskim who lived approximately during the 11th to 15th centuries, in the era before the writing of the Shulchan Aruch, and following the *Geonim*.

Rosh Chodesh seuda- Festive meal for the new Jewish month

Rosh Hashanah- Jewish New Year

Rosh Yeshiva- Head *rabbi* of a *yeshivah*

Ruach Hakodesh- Divine Inspiration

Ruchniyus'dike- See **Ruchniyos**

Schmooze/Schmoozing- Talking and hanging out
Sefer/Seforim- Book(s)
Segulah- Remedy or charm
Seraphim- Angels
Seudah- Festive meal
Shaaloh- Question for a Rav to avoid stumbling on another occasion
Sha'atnez- The prohibition against wearing clothes woven of wool and flax.
Shabbosdiker kapota- Shabbos garment
Shabbos- The Jewish Sabbath, a day of rest and spiritual enrichment.
Shacharis- Morning daily prayer service
Shaliach- Messenger
Shalom Aleichem- Greating in Hebrew meaning "peace be upon you"
Shalosh Seudos- Third festive meal on Shabbos
Shamash/Shammes- Lit. servant. 1) The candle that is used to light other Chanukkah candles; 2) the janitor or caretaker of a synagogue
Shamayim- Heaven
Shas Bavli and Yerushalmi- Bavli Talmud compiled in Bavel, Jerusalem Talmud compiled in Jerusalem before the Bavli Talmud
Shas- Complete order of the entire Talmud
Shavuos- Holiday commemorating the giving of the Torah
Shechinah- The Divine Presence
Shechitah- Slaughter of *kosher* animals
Sheker- Falsehood
Shemoneh Esreh- The central prayer of the Jewish liturgy
Shidduch- Dating through a matchmaker
Shikkur- Drunk
Shir Hama'alos- Song of Ascents in the Psalms
Shiras Hashirim- A Song written by King Solomon
Shiur- Torah class
Shliach- Messenger
Shlep- Drag around
Shochtim- Slaughterers of kosher animals
Shtiblach- Small synagogues
Shtreimel- Fur hat worn during *Shabbos*
Shul- Synagogue
Shulchan Aruch- Code of Jewish Law
Siddur- Prayer book
Simchah- Joy and celebration
Simchas Torah- Holiday Celebrating the Torah
Sippurei Tzaddikim- Stories of righteous people
Siyum- Party for finishing a Torah book
Sod- Secret of the Torah
Succos/Succah- Jewish Holiday celebrated in booths
Tallis- Prayer shawl
Talmid- Student
Talmud Chacham- Wise student
Tanach- Acronym of Torah (Law), Nevi'im (Prophets) and Ketuvim (Writings)
Tanna- Jewish sages whose views were recorded in the Mishnah in the first and second centuries

Tefila / Tefilos- Prayer(s)
Tefillin- Holy Scriptures wrapped in a box with leather straps to attach to the head and arm
Tehillim- Psalms
Teshuva- Repentance
Tikkun- Repairing
Tikun Chatzos- (lit. "Midnight service"); a prayer recited by pious Jews at midnight, lamenting the destruction of the Holy Temple
Tishah b' Av- Memorial Day to recall the destruction of the Temple
Toiveled- Purified oneself in the Mikvah
Tzaddik/Tzaddkim- Lit. Righteous person(s). A completely righteous person often believed to have special, mystical power.
Tzaddik Nistar- Hidden righteous man
Tzedakah- Charity
Tzetl- Note
Yechidus- Personal time spent with one's rebbe
Yeshiva- School for learning Torah for older boys or men
Yeshuah- Redemption
Yetzer hara- Evil inclination
Yichus- Family Background
Yid / Yiddala / Yidden – Jew (s) in Yiddish
Yiddishkeit- Yiddish for Judaism
Yiras Shamayim- Fear of G-D
Yom Tov- Holiday
Yungeleit / Yungerman- Yiddish for young man
Zechus- Merit
Zeide- Grandfather
Zemanim- Times of the day

Made in the USA
Coppell, TX
21 December 2020